The Professional Edition

Relentless Pursuit

The Foundation And Principles of
Game Theory for Negotiating

Stephen L. Nalley DBA., CHA

American Business Magnate, Entrepreneur, Veteran and Author

Dedication

"This book is dedicated to my oldest daughter Breanna Nalley for the constant light you bring into my world, your unwavering support, and the boundless inspiration you spark within me.

Every page I write is a testament to the strength and grace you exude daily. In all that I do, you are my guiding star.."

Acknowledgment

I would like to acknowledge everyone who has ever wronged me, betrayed me, doubted me, gave up on me and/or ever tried to cheat me. You are my compelling "WHY" that has driven me to such heights. Your hate, negativity and disrespect has always motivated me to barrel through any setback and every adversity I have ever faced in my life.

I would never have set the bar so high and gone so far if it were not for you and your actions. You know who you are, and I would like to thank you all for providing me with the inspiration that I needed to drive my passion and achieve my own definition of success in my life.

About the Author

Stephen Nalley is an American Business Magnate, Entrepreneur, Investor, Veteran and Author. He is best known as the principal founder of Inner Circle Capital, Breanna Bailey Investments and Black Briar Advisors.

Over the course of Nalley's 30-year professional career, he has started and/or participated in hundreds of corporate ventures and managed over $2 Billion in Real Estate Assets.

Prior to his professional pursuits, Nalley served his country honorably in the United States Army as a Non-Commission Officer and Commando with the Army's Elite 10th Mountain Division.

After serving his Country, Nalley went on to obtain academic degrees from several prestigious colleges. Nalley earned a Bachelor of Science Degree in Healthcare Administration from the University of North Florida, Master's Degree in Business Administration and Doctorate Degree in Business Administration from the University of Atlanta and a Law Degree from the Washington University School of Law.

Stephen is a Certified Hotel Administrator through the American Hotel & Lodging Association and is a Member of the Forbes Business Council, as well as, a Writer for the Entrepreneur Leadership Network

Preface

In the vast tapestry of human interaction, few threads are as intricate and compelling as those woven by game theory. This fascinating branch of mathematics and social science dives deep into our decision-making processes, illuminating the strategies we employ when faced with choices that not only impact us but also others around us.

As you delve into the pages of this book, you'll encounter scenarios that might feel plucked straight from your daily life: from the tense moments of diplomatic negotiations to the more relatable and intimate crossroads in personal relationships.

We journey from the classic Prisoner's Dilemma to the Dance of the Cournot Competition and touch upon lesser-known but equally compelling constructs like the Stag Hunt and the Traveler's Dilemma. While the games themselves might be theoretical, the insights they offer into human nature are profoundly real.

Yet, this book isn't just a deep dive into abstract theories. Interwoven with these academic explorations are real-world applications: how businesses merge, how price wars are sparked, how nations converse, and even how individual relationships ebb and flow.

By grounding these concepts in real-life scenarios, we not only gain a better understanding of game theory but also a more profound appreciation for the complex ballet of human interactions.

As we navigate this journey together, I hope you'll find yourself not just understanding game theory more deeply but also looking at the decisions and negotiations of your own life with newfound insight. Thank you for embarking on this exploration with me.

Contents

10 | Page

Page Left Blank Intentionally

Chapter 1

Game Theory and Its Application to Negotiation

"In the intricate ballet of negotiation, game theory serves as the choreography, guiding each step towards a harmonious finale."

Introduction

In an interconnected world, our decisions often intertwine with the choices made by others. From global political treaties to business deals, the subtle dance of negotiation is omnipresent. Understanding this dance is paramount for anyone aiming to navigate these waters effectively. At the intersection of mathematics, economics, and psychology lies game theory, a powerful tool that seeks to understand strategic decision-making when multiple players interact. This book delves into the world of game theory and examines its profound impact on negotiation, illuminating how its principles can be harnessed to achieve optimal outcomes.

Introduction to Game Theory

Game theory can be thought of as the science of strategy. It doesn't simply analyze how decisions are made but delves into how decisions should be made when faced with an adversary or partner whose actions are interdependent with one's own. This intertwining of decision-making processes is what gives game theory its name, turning real-world scenarios into "games" that can be dissected and understood.

Definition and History

Definition

Game theory is a mathematical study of decision-making in situations where multiple players must make choices that potentially affect the interests of others. These 'games' can range from two people deciding on a joint activity to complex interactions within marketplaces or international politics.

Historical Context

Game theory's foundational roots can be traced back to the 18th century, but it truly blossomed in the 20th century. The seminal work "Theory of Games and Economic Behavior" (1944) by John von Neumann and Oskar Morgenstern is often regarded as the cornerstone of modern game theory. However, it was John Nash's development of the Nash Equilibrium, a situation in which each player in a game chooses the optimal strategy in response to the choices of other players, that pushed game theory to the forefront of economic thought. Over the decades, this discipline has been enriched by contributions from economists, mathematicians, psychologists, and more, each bringing unique perspectives.

Basics of Strategic Interaction

Game theory is grounded in the understanding of strategic interactions, which occur whenever the outcome of one's choices depends on the choices made by others. Here are some foundational concepts:

Players: The decision-makers in the game.

Strategies: The plan of action a player decides upon. It defines what a player will do in every possible situation.

Payoffs: A numerical representation of the outcomes in the game. In essence, it quantifies a player's preferences over possible outcomes.

Nash Equilibrium: A situation in which every player's strategy maximizes their payoff given the strategies the others have chosen. No player has an incentive to deviate from their strategy.

Dominant and Dominated Strategies: A strategy is dominant if its payoff is always better than any other strategy, no matter what the other players do. Conversely, a strategy is dominated if there is some other strategy that always yields a better payoff, regardless of what the other players are doing.

Importance in Negotiation

Negotiations, whether they occur in boardrooms, marketplaces, or international arenas, are rife with strategic interactions. Understanding the principles of game theory can offer valuable insights into the negotiation process:

Predicting Outcomes: With game theory, negotiators can better predict the likely outcomes of different strategies, helping to inform their decisions.

Understanding Mutual Dependencies: Game theory highlights how the decisions of one party depend on the choices of others. Recognizing these interdependencies can lead to more informed and collaborative negotiations.

Overcoming Deadlocks: Deadlocks in negotiations, where mutual decisions lead to suboptimal outcomes, can be better understood and resolved with the help of game theory. For instance, the classic Prisoner's Dilemma provides insight into why two rational individuals might not cooperate, even if it appears that cooperation is in their best interest.

Efficient Bargaining: Game theory can guide negotiators towards bargaining solutions that are both efficient (leading to the largest combined benefit for all parties) and fair.

Ethical Considerations: Game theory can also shed light on ethical considerations in negotiations. For instance, the Ultimatum Game, where one player decides how to divide a sum of money and the other chooses to accept or reject the offer, underscores the human preference for fairness over strict rationality.

Conclusion

Game theory stands as a beacon in the complex world of strategic decision-making, providing a systematic approach to understanding the myriad interactions that shape our world. For negotiators, game theory isn't just a theoretical construct; it's a practical tool that can lead to better decisions, more favorable outcomes, and a deeper understanding of the interplay between different parties. As we continue to advance in an interconnected world, the principles of game theory will undoubtedly play an increasingly pivotal role in guiding the art and science of negotiation.

Chapter 2

Foundations of Game Theory

"In the grand theater of decision-making, the foundations of game theory set the stage, where players, strategies, payoffs, and equilibria come together in asymphony of choices and outcomes."

Introduction

The vast realm of decision-making often transcends solitary actions, intertwining with the choices of others. This intricate dance of decisions, reliant on interdependence, is governed by the principles of game theory-a sophisticated field that systematically examines strategic interactions among rational decision-makers.

This chapter delves into the foundational components of game theory, dissecting the roles of players, strategies, and payoffs, and illustrating the significance of concepts like Nash Equilibrium and dominant strategies.

Foundations of Game Theory

Game theory, at its heart, is the mathematical study of strategies for dealing with competitive situations where the outcome of a participant's choice of action depends critically on the actions of other participants.

Its foundational tenets lie in defining the participants, understanding their choices, and examining the resulting outcomes.

Players: The Decision-Makers
Every game in game theory is defined by its players-the entities making decisions. These can be individuals, groups, companies, or even nations, depending on the scenario being modeled.

Characteristics of Players

Rationality: Players are assumed to be rational, meaning they aim to maximize their own payoffs.

Preferences: Every player has clear preferences, allowing them to rank different outcomes. Strategizing Ability: Players can contemplate the strategies of others, even thinking multiple steps ahead.

Strategies: The Choices at Hand
A strategy represents the set plan of action a player will follow throughout the game. It specifies what a player will do in every possible situation.

Types of Strategies

Pure Strategies: A strategy that provides a specific action for every possible situation.

Mixed Strategies: A strategy where a player makes a random choice among two or more possible actions based on a certain probability distribution.

Payoffs: The Outcomes of Decisions
Payoffs represent the outcomes resulting from the combination of strategies chosen by all players. It quantifies the benefit (or cost) each player receives from each possible combination of strategies.

Characteristics of Payoffs

Quantifiable: Even if the outcome is qualitative (e.g., satisfaction, happiness), it's represented with a numerical value.

Orderable: Players can rank outcomes in order of preference.

Transitive: If one outcome is preferred over a second, and the second is preferred over a third, the first is preferred over the third.

Nash Equilibrium: Where Best Responses Meet
Coined after John Nash, a Nash Equilibrium occurs when every player's strategy is optimal given the strategies chosen by the other players. In essence, when a game reaches Nash Equilibrium, no player has an incentive to deviate from their strategy, knowing the strategies of the others.

Characteristics and Implications

Stability: At Nash Equilibrium, the game is stable since no player stands to gain by changing their strategy unilaterally.

Existence: John Nash proved that every finite game

(with a finite number of players and strategies) has at least one Nash Equilibrium.

Multiplicity: Some games have multiple Nash Equilibria, leading to different potential stable outcomes.

Dominant and Dominated Strategies: Optimal Choices and Redundancies

Dominant Strategy: A strategy is dominant if it consistently results in the best possible payoff for a player, no matter what the other players do. When every player in a game has a dominant strategy, the game will always result in the same outcome.

Dominated Strategy: Conversely, a dominated strategy is one that, regardless of what any other players do, results in the lowest payoff for a player. Rational players will not use dominated strategies.

Implications: Reduction of Complexity: By identifying and eliminating dominated strategies, analysts can reduce the complexity of some games, making them easier to analyze.

Predictability: In games where dominant strategies exist for all players, the outcome becomes predictable.

Conclusion

The interplay of decisions, strategies, and outcomes underpins the multifaceted world of game theory. By understanding its foundational elements-players, strategies, payoffs, and key concepts like Nash

Equilibrium and dominant strategies-we gain valuable insights into the intricacies of strategic decision-making. Whether it's nations forging treaties, corporations making strategic moves, or individuals interacting in daily life, the principles of game theory offer a structured lens to understand, predict, and optimize interactions in an interconnected world.

Chapter 3

The Prisoner's Dilemma

"In the maze of choices that life presents, the Prisoner's Dilemma stands as a testament to the complexities of trust and strategy, urging us to think beyond the immediate and embrace the vastness of implications and iterations."

Introduction

The realm of game theory is riddled with fascinating insights into the strategic interactions between rational players. Among these, the Prisoner's Dilemma stands out as one of the most influential and widely analyzed.

This chapter delves deep into the Prisoner's Dilemma, exploring its background, structure, and implications, particularly in the context of negotiations. Furthermore, we will examine the nuances of its iterated version and immerse in practical exercises to better understand the dynamics of this fundamental game.

Background and Structure

Origin of the Prisoner's Dilemma: The Prisoner's Dilemma is often framed around the story of two suspects arrested for a crime. While the police lack concrete evidence for a major charge, they have enough to convict both on a minor charge.

Core Structure

The police offer each prisoner a deal: if one testifies (defects) against the other and the other remains silent (cooperates), the defector goes free while the silent accomplice receives the full sentence. If both remain silent, both serve a short sentence. If both defect, both serve a medium-length sentence. The dilemma arises because, while the best collective outcome is for both to stay silent, individual rationality pushes each prisoner to defect.

Key Takeaways from the Structure

Dominant Strategy: For each prisoner, the dominant strategy is to defect, as it always results in a better outcome regardless of the other's choice. Collective Suboptimality: When both prisoners follow their dominant strategies, they end up in a situation that's worse for both compared to mutual cooperation.

Iterated Prisoner's Dilemma

While the traditional Prisoner's Dilemma is a one-shot game, real-world scenarios often involve players encountering each other repeatedly. This leads to the iterated version, where the game is played multiple times in succession.

Characteristics and Outcomes

Memory Matters: Players remember previous moves and adjust their strategies.

Tit-for-Tat: A commonly adopted strategy where a player starts by cooperating and then mimics the opponent's last move. This strategy has been found to be particularly effective in numerous computer-simulated tournaments.

Emergence of Cooperation: In iterated versions, there's a higher likelihood of cooperative behavior emerging, especially when players value future rewards.

Implications in Negotiations

The Prisoner's Dilemma offers invaluable lessons for negotiations:

Trust and Collaboration: Just as mutual cooperation yields better outcomes for the prisoners, negotiations often benefit from mutual trust and collaboration.

Short-term vs. Long-term: While defecting can provide immediate gains (akin to winning a single round of the Prisoner's Dilemma), long-term relationships in negotiations can resemble the iterated version, where consistent defection can lead to mutual losses.

Communication's Role: In the Prisoner's Dilemma, lack of communication between the two prisoners is a core problem. In negotiations, effective communication can help parties realize and achieve mutually beneficial outcomes.

Practical Exercises & Analysis

Exercise 1: Classroom Iterated Prisoner's Dilemma
Setup: Students pair up and play ten rounds of the Prisoner's Dilemma, noting down choices and outcomes.

Analysis: Discussion follows about patterns observed, strategies adopted, and the evolution of decisions. Most students will likely shift from defection towards more cooperative strategies as rounds progress.

Exercise 2: Business Negotiation Simulation
Setup: Participants simulate a business negotiation where two companies decide to cooperate (e.g., share resources) or defect (e.g., launch competing products). Outcomes are quantified in terms of hypothetical profit.

Analysis: Discussions can revolve around the perceived benefits of defection versus long-term cooperation, the role of communication, and strategies for fostering trust.

Exercise 3: Role-play Real-world Scenarios
Setup: Participants are given real-world scenarios, such as countries deciding on environmental regulations, where mutual cooperation is beneficial but defection has short-term gains.

Analysis: By placing participants in real-world decision-making positions, the exercise provides insights into the complexities and pressures that lead to decisions resembling the Prisoner's Dilemma.

Conclusion

The Prisoner's Dilemma, in its simplicity, encapsulates profound truths about strategic decision-making, trust, and the interplay between individual and collective rationality. While on the surface, it might appear as a mere theoretical construct, its implications permeate various aspects of human interaction, particularly in negotiations.

By understanding and appreciating the dynamics of the Prisoner's Dilemma, one can not only navigate the complex world of strategic interactions more effectively but also foster a deeper sense of collaboration and mutual benefit in negotiations and beyond.

Prisoner's Dilemma Practical Application and Analysis

Business Mergers: A Prisoner's Dilemma Exploration

Scenario: Two major tech firms, AlphaTech and BetaSoft, stand at the precipice of a merger that promises to reshape the tech landscape. Central to their negotiations are confidential R&D projects. Sharing these projects can streamline post-merger integration, while withholding can offer competitive advantages if the merger collapses. Both firms face a pivotal decision.

Game Setup:

Players: AlphaTech & BetaSoft

Choices:
Share R&D
Withhold R&D

Payoff Matrix:

	BetaSoft Shares	BetaSoft Withholds
AlphaTech Shares	(Integration Benefit, Integration Benefit)	(Competitive Loss, Competitive Gain)
AlphaTech Withholds	(Competitive Gain, Competitive Loss)	(Status Quo, Status Quo)

Explanation of Outcomes:

Both Share (Integration Benefit, Integration Benefit):
- o Both companies share their R&D projects.
- o The merger integrates smoothly, leading to increased market share, faster innovation, and a strengthened position in the market.
- o Trust between the companies is solidified, which might lead to more collaborative opportunities in the future.

AlphaTech Shares, BetaSoft Withholds (Competitive Loss, Competitive Gain):
- o AlphaTech's willingness to share without reciprocity leaves them vulnerable.
- o BetaSoft gains a competitive edge by accessing AlphaTech's R&D, giving them leverage in future dealings or a significant advantage if the merger collapses. Trust is eroded, potentially endangering the merger's long-term success.

AlphaTech Withholds, BetaSoft Shares (Competitive Gain, Competitive Loss):
- o Roles are reversed from the second scenario.
- o AlphaTech gains the upper hand, accessing BetaSoft's R&D without giving away their own.

Both Withhold (Status Quo, Status Quo):
- o Neither firm gains an advantage, but they also don't benefit from shared innovation.
- o The merger might still proceed, but without the streamlined integration that shared R&D would have facilitated.
- o The relationship remains neutral, with neither trust gained nor eroded.

Strategic Implications

If both firms believe the other will act in good faith and share, they'll achieve the best mutual outcome. However, the temptation to gain a competitive edge might lead a firm to withhold, especially if they believe the other firm will share.

The safest play (to avoid potential competitive loss) is for both to withhold, but this prevents the mutual benefits of sharing.

Conclusion

The Prisoner's Dilemma encapsulates the strategic challenges AlphaTech and BetaSoft face. While mutual cooperation (sharing R&D) leads to the best combined outcome, the individual temptation or fear might prevent this optimal scenario. Their decisions will not only shape the immediate aftermath of the merger but also set the tone for future collaborations or competitions.

Prisoner's Dilemma Practical Application and Analysis

Lease Agreements: The Prisoner's Dilemma Between Alex and Blake

Scenario

In the heart of the bustling city, roommates Alex and Blake are on the cusp of a crucial decision. Their lease renewal is looming, and though the modern flat has served them well, both harbor dreams of new locales and fresh starts. Yet, the prospect of higher rent acts as a deterrent. The catch? If both renew the lease, they benefit from a special discount. But if one departs, leaving the other behind, the lone tenant will grapple with a rent spike. The conundrum unfolds as the duo grapples with individual desires versus collective financial prudence.

Game Setup:

Players: Alex & Blake

Choices:
Renew (R)
Move Out (M)

Payoff Matrix (Described in terms of individual financial burdens):

	Blake Renews	Blake Moves Out
Alex Renews	Discounted Rent for Both (-Low Burden,-LowBurden)	High Rent for Alex (-High Burden, No Burden)
Alex Moves Out	High Rent for Blake (-High Burden, No Burden)	Both Move to Different Places (No Burden, No Burden)

Explanation of Outcomes:

Both Renew (R, R):
- o Recognizing the monetary benefits of the discount, both Alex and Blake decide to renew their lease.
- o Each incurs a lower financial burden due to the reduced rent, even though their personal desires lean towards moving out.

Alex Renews, Blake Moves Out (R, M):
- o Alex, prioritizing the financial aspect, decides to renew, hoping that Blake does the same.
- o Blake, however, chooses to move out.
- o Alex now faces the high rent alone, making his financial burden heavy, while Blake, free from the lease, bears no rent-related burden.

Alex Moves Out, Blake Renews (M, R):
- o Blake decides to stay, betting on the discount

when renewing with Alex.
- o Alex, wanting a change of scenery, moves out.
- o The outcome mirrors the previous scenario but with roles reversed: Blake now has the heavy financial burden, while Alex is free of the lease.

Both Move Out (M, M):
- o Both Alex and Blake, acting on their desire for change, decide to move to different locations.
- o Neither incurs any rent-related burden from the old apartment, but they forego the potential discount and face the uncertainties and potential costs of new living arrangements.

Strategic Implications

The Prisoner's Dilemma underscores the tension between individual desires and collective outcomes. In this scenario, both Alex and Blake face a trade-off between personal aspirations and potential financial benefits.

Communication can significantly impact the decision. If Alex and Blake had openly discussed their intentions and desires, they might have made more informed choices.

Conclusion

The lease renewal scenario with Alex and Blake brings the intricacies of decision-making to the fore. The Prisoner's Dilemma aptly captures the essence of their choices: pursuing individual goals or making sacrifices for collective benefits. While they opted for the latter, the underlying dilemma remains universal and relatable, revealing the complex dance between personal desires and shared outcomes.

Chapter 4

The Matching Penny Game

"In the delicate balance of decisions, the Matching Pennies Game reminds us that sometimes, success isn't just about predicting the world around us, but also the ever-evolving dance of opposing choices and the search for equilibrium."

Introduction

Within the domain of game theory, several models and simulations exemplify the intricate dance of decision-making, strategy, and outcomes. Among such models, the Matching Pennies Game stands as a straightforward yet illuminating representation of strategic interactions, particularly in zero-sum scenarios.

This chapter dives deep into the essence of the Matching Pennies Game, its equilibrium dynamics, its resonance in zero-sum negotiations, and how its principles can be practically applied and analyzed.

Definition and Dynamics

The Basic Setup

The Matching Pennies Game involves two players, each with a penny. They simultaneously decide to show either the 'Heads' or 'Tails' side. If the pennies match (both Heads or both Tails), one player wins, and the other loses. If the pennies are opposite, the reverse happens.

Characteristics

Symmetry: The game is symmetric; both players have the same strategy set and opposite payoffs.

Pure Strategies: In the realm of pure strategies, no player has a dominant or dominated strategy. Whether a player chooses Heads or Tails, the expected payoff will depend entirely on the unpredictable choice of the opponent.

Mixed Strategy Equilibrium:
Given the absence of a dominant strategy in the Matching Pennies Game, the focus shifts to mixed strategies, where players randomize their choices based on a certain probability distribution.

Equilibrium Dynamics

Randomization: For each player, the optimal strategy is to randomize their choice, making them unpredictable. This involves choosing Heads or Tails with a probability of 0.5 each.

Nash Equilibrium: The mixed strategy Nash Equilibrium occurs when both players choose Heads and Tails with equal probability. At this equilibrium, knowing the strategy of the opponent doesn't provide any advantage since the opponent's actions remain unpredictable.

Relevance to Zero-Sum Negotiations

The Matching Pennies Game is fundamentally a zero-sum game; one player's gain is the other's loss. This intrinsic characteristic makes it particularly relevant to situations of direct competition, where mutual gains are impossible.

Implications in Negotiations

Unpredictability: In zero-sum scenarios, like competitive bids or auctions, maintaining unpredictability can be essential to prevent being outmaneuvered by opponents.

No Win-Win: Unlike many negotiation scenarios where mutual benefits can be achieved, zero-sum negotiations reflected by the Matching Pennies dynamic emphasize the competition over a fixed pie.

Strategic Flexibility: Relying on a single strategy or approach can be detrimental in zero-sum negotiations. As exemplified by the game, flexibility and randomization can often yield better outcomes.

Practical Exercises & Analysis

Exercise 1: Live Matching Pennies Tournament

Setup: Participants pair up and play multiple rounds of Matching Pennies, recording outcomes.

Analysis: Discussion can revolve around the strategies adopted, any patterns observed, and the difficulty in maintaining true unpredictability.

Exercise 2: Modified Business Scenario

Setup: Two businesses are deciding pricing strategies. If they choose similar prices, one business (with a better marketing campaign) wins the majority of the market share. If they choose different pricing strategies, the business with the lower price gains the market.

Analysis: Participants can discuss real-world implications, challenges in randomizing business strategies, and the potential benefits of moving away from a zero-sum dynamic.

Exercise 3: Role-play in Auction Scenarios

Setup: Participants simulate an auction scenario where two bidders aim to win a valuable contract. While the highest bid wins, if both bid similarly, external factors like company reputation might determine the winner.

Analysis: This activity can lead to discussions on the

risks and rewards of aggressive vs. conservative bidding, the challenge of predicting competitor moves, and the broader implications of zero-sum dynamics in business.

Conclusion

The Matching Pennies Game, in its elegant simplicity, encapsulates the nuances of zero-sum interactions and the strategic challenges therein. While the game might appear trivial at first glance, its layers of complexity resonate deeply in scenarios of direct competition and negotiation. By understanding the core dynamics and equilibrium of the game, individuals and entities can better navigate competitive landscapes, appreciating the value of unpredictability and the ever-present dance of strategy and counter-strategy.

Matching Penny Practical Application and Analysis

Vendor Agreements: The Matching Penny Game Between Company A and Vendor B

Scenario

Amidst the hustle and bustle of industry, Company A, a burgeoning manufacturer, is looking to secure materials for its upcoming production run. Vendor B holds the key, boasting the resources Company A needs.

The dance begins with Company A's aspiration for bulk rates. Vendor B, while having the capacity to offer bulk rates, remains undecided - weighing the possibility of maximizing profits with regular prices against the allure of securing a loyal, bulk-buying client. The stakes?

If Vendor B fails to match Company A's expectations, they might just lose a valuable client to competitors.

Game Setup:

Players: Company A & Vendor B

Choices:
Expect/Offer Bulk Rate (B)
Expect/Offer Regular Rate (R)

Payoff Matrix (Described in terms of the satisfaction/profit for Company A and Vendor B):

	Vendor B Offers Bulk Rate	Vendor B Offers Regular Rate
Company A Expects Bulk Rate	Mutual Satisfaction (High, High)	Company A Looks Elsewhere (Low, Medium)
Company A Expects Regular Rate	Missed Savings, Vendor B's Lower Profit (Medium, Low)	Mutual Understanding (Medium, Medium)

Explanation of Outcomes

Both Align on Bulk Rate (B, B):
- o Company A, expecting a bulk rate, aligns perfectly with Vendor B's offer.
- o This results in high satisfaction for Company A due to savings, and Vendor B secures a potentially loyal client, translating to high satisfaction.

Mismatch: Company A Expects Bulk, Vendor B Offers Regular (B, R):
- o Company A, hoping for a bulk discount, is met with Vendor B's regular rates.
- o Disappointed by the mismatch in expectations, Company A considers looking for another vendor. Vendor B gains a medium profit but risks losing future business.

Mismatch: Company A Expects Regular, Vendor B Offers Bulk (R, B):

- Vendor B, in an attempt to woo Company A, offers a bulk rate, but Company A was only expecting the regular rate.
- Company A benefits from unexpected savings, but Vendor B has low profits due to the unplanned discount.

Both Align on Regular Rate (R, R):

- Company A, expecting regular rates, matches Vendor B's offer perfectly.
- This results in a medium level of satisfaction for both parties - a balanced outcome where expectations align, but there's no special gain for either side.

Strategic Implications

The Matching Penny game emphasizes the importance of predicting the opponent's move. Here, the "game" is to align on rates, and any mismatch could affect future business relationships.

Open communication and understanding market norms can help in aligning expectations, though the inherent uncertainty in negotiations remains.

Conclusion

The delicate dance between Company A and Vendor B in their quest to align on pricing illuminates the complexities of business negotiations. The Matching Penny game, in this context, underscores the challenges of prediction, the nuances of strategy, and the balance of risks and rewards. As both entities navigate their interests, the outcome remains uncertain - a testament to the ever-evolving nature of business interactions.

Matching Penny Practical Application and Analysis

Contract Negotiations: The Matching Penny Game Between the Author and the Publishing House

Scenario

In a sunlit room, an intense negotiation is unfolding. The author, acclaimed for her bestsellers, wants a deserving royalty for her upcoming masterpiece. Opposite her sits the representative of Prestige Publish, a top publishing house.

Both parties know the stakes: the royalty percentage must align for the deal to go through. If their demands and offers don't match, the literary world might miss out on a potential classic.

Game Setup

Players: Author & Prestige Publish

Choices:
High (H)
Low (L)

Payoff Matrix:

	PrestigePublish offers High	**PrestigePublish offers Low**
Author demands High	Deal (Win, Win)	No Deal (Lose, Win)
Author demands Low	No Deal (Win, Lose)	Deal (Lose, Lose)

(Note: In the Matching Penny game, the goal of one player is to match the other player's decision, while the other player aims to mismatch. In this adapted version, both parties aim to match.)

Explanation of Outcomes

Both Opt for High (Deal, Win-Win):
- o Recognizing the potential success of the book and the value the author brings, PrestigePublish offers a high royalty.
- o The author, having demanded a high royalty, sees her expectations met.
- o Both parties win. The book deal is secured, ensuring both financial and reputational gains.

Author Demands High, PrestigePublish offers Low (No Deal, Lose-Win):
- o The author expects a high royalty based on her previous successes and the quality of her new work.

- PrestigePublish, perhaps aiming to maximize its profits or underestimating the book's potential, offers a lower royalty.
- The mismatch leads to no deal. The author is likely to explore other publishers, and while PrestigePublish saves on royalty, they lose a potential bestseller.

Author Demands Low, PrestigePublish offers High (No Deal, Win-Lose):
- Underestimating her market value or simply wishing for a quick deal, the author is willing to settle for a lower royalty.
- PrestigePublish, valuing the author's work, is prepared to offer a higher percentage.
- The mismatch leads to no immediate deal, though this scenario offers room for further negotiation. The author realizes she can demand more, and PrestigePublish might adjust its offer accordingly.

Both Opt for Low (Deal, Lose-Lose):
- The author, for reasons like wanting a guaranteed quick publication, is willing to accept a lower royalty.
- PrestigePublish, looking to minimize costs, offers a low royalty.
- They strike a deal, but both parties lose in terms of potential value. The author receives less than she might have, and PrestigePublish signals that they don't fully value the work, which could affect future negotiations or the marketing effort for the book.

Strategic Implications

The Matching Penny framework emphasizes the importance of alignment in negotiations. Both parties need to understand the other's values, expectations, and the broader market dynamics.

Information asymmetry can lead to mismatches. Open communication can help bridge gaps and lead to win-win scenarios.

Conclusion

Contract negotiations, especially in creative fields like publishing, are a delicate dance of value assessment, market dynamics, and interpersonal understanding. The Matching Penny game, as applied to the author and Prestige Publish, underscores the necessity of alignment in expectations and offers. While mismatches can be roadblocks, they can also serve as stepping stones to mutual understanding and successful collaboration.

Chapter 5

Deadlock in Negotiations

"In the chessboard of negotiations, a deadlock is not a checkmate but a pause, challenging us to reflect on causes, weigh the consequences, and craft innovative strategies to move forward."

Introduction

Negotiations form an integral part of our personal, professional, and political spheres. Often seen as the interplay of communication, strategy, and mutual benefit, negotiations, however, don't always go as smoothly as one would hope.

A common challenge faced in negotiations is a deadlock - a point where discussions seem to halt without reaching a resolution. This chapter delves into the intricacies of deadlocks, exploring their causes, consequences, and, crucially, how game theory can offer tools to navigate and potentially overcome them.

Causes and Consequences of Deadlock in Negotiations Understanding the Deadlock: At its core, a deadlock is a standstill in a negotiation where all parties believe they have exhausted their available options and yet fail to reach an agreement.

Common Causes
Fixed Pie Perception: Both parties believe that the resource under negotiation is fixed, leading to a zero-

sum mindset.

Information Asymmetry: Parties might be withholding information, thinking it gives them an advantage, but it ends up preventing a mutual understanding.

Commitment to Positions: Parties become so anchored to their initial positions that they become inflexible, preventing exploration of potential compromises.

Emotional Factors: Past conflicts, mistrust, or simple ego clashes can hinder objective discussions. Consequences:

Missed Opportunities: When negotiations stall, both parties might miss out on mutually beneficial opportunities.

Wasted Resources: Time, effort, and even monetary resources spent on negotiations end up being wasted.

Strained Relationships: Deadlocks can strain future interactions, making subsequent negotiations even tougher.

Overcoming Deadlock Using Game Theory

Game theory, with its mathematical and logical frameworks, provides tools to understand the dynamics of deadlocks better and identify potential paths forward.

Applying Game Theory

Identifying Dominant Strategies: Understanding if one party has a dominant strategy (a strategy that's the best choice regardless of what the other party does) can help in predicting and preventing deadlocks.

Seeking Nash Equilibrium: Finding a point where both parties' strategies are optimized in response to one another can lead to potential resolutions.

Iterative Games & Reputation: In repeated negotiations, parties can use the outcomes of past games (previous negotiations) to build trust and reputation, thus mitigating the chances of a deadlock.

Strategic Moves to Break the Deadlock

Using game theory as a foundation, various strategic moves can be employed to break or prevent deadlocks.

Expanding the Pie: Moving away from a zero-sum mindset and looking for ways to increase the overall value under negotiation.

Role Reversal: Parties swap positions and argue from the other's perspective, leading to greater empathy and understanding.

Third-party Mediation: Introducing a neutral third party can help break impasses by offering fresh perspectives or facilitating communication.

Segmentation: Breaking down the negotiation into smaller parts, resolving easier issues first, can create a momentum of agreement.

Postponement: Taking a break and revisiting the negotiation after a while can help in diffusing tensions and bringing in new perspectives.

Practical Exercises & Analysis

Exercise 1: Role-play Negotiation Scenario

Setup: Participants are given a scenario where two businesses are negotiating a partnership but have hit a deadlock over terms of profit sharing.

Analysis: Post-exercise, a discussion can ensue about what caused the deadlock, how participants felt, and what strategies they employed or could have employed.

Exercise 2: The Ultimatum Game

Setup: A classic game in behavioral economics where one player proposes how to split a sum of money, and the other accepts or rejects. If rejected, both get nothing.

Analysis: The game can highlight how fairness perceptions can lead to deadlocks (rejections) even at personal costs.

Exercise 3: Iterative Business Negotiation Simulation

Setup: Businesses negotiate contracts over multiple rounds, with outcomes of one round affecting subsequent rounds.

Analysis: Discussions can revolve around the emergence of trust, how past deadlocks influenced future negotiations, and strategies that emerged organically over iterations.

Conclusion

Deadlocks in negotiations, while challenging, aren't insurmountable barriers. With an understanding of their causes and consequences, coupled with strategic insights from game theory, negotiators can be better equipped to navigate these standstills.

By adopting flexible strategies, seeking mutual benefits, and continually striving for communication and understanding, even the most challenging deadlocks can transform into opportunities for collaboration and mutual growth.

Deadlock Practical Application and Analysis

Hostage Crisis: The Deadlock Between Terrorists and the Government

Scenario

The air is thick with tension as a city grapples with an unforeseen hostage crisis. A group of terrorists has taken innocent citizens captive, leveraging their safety for a hefty ransom.

On the other side stands the government, resolute and unwavering in its policy: no negotiations with terrorists. The stakes are high, and neither party seems willing to budge, resulting in a palpable deadlock. Time is of the essence, and with each passing moment, the atmosphere grows increasingly volatile.

Game Setup:

Players: Terrorists & Government

Choices:
Stand Firm (SF)
Concede (C)

Payoff Matrix (Described in terms of the successful achievement of goals for both the Terrorists and the Government):

	Government Stands Firm	Government Concedes
Terrorists Stand Firm	Stalemate, Danger Escalates (Low, Low)	Terrorists' Demands Met (High, Very Low)
Terrorists Concede	Hostages Freed, No Ransom Paid (Low, High)	Hostages Freed, Ransom Paid (Medium, Medium)

Explanation of Outcomes

Both Sides Stand Firm (SF, SF):
Neither the terrorists nor the government budge from their positions.
- o The standoff becomes more protracted and dangerous, with the safety of the hostages hanging in the balance.

Government Concedes, Terrorists Stand Firm (SF, C):
- o The government, assessing the gravity of the situation, decides to pay the ransom, while the terrorists remain resolute in their demands.
- o This results in the hostages being released, but the terrorists' demands are met, setting a potential precedent for future incidents.

Terrorists Concede, Government Stands Firm (C, SF):

- The terrorists, possibly due to internal pressures or realizing the futility of their demands against an unyielding government, release the hostages without receiving any ransom.
- The government's policy is upheld, and the hostages are safe, but the potential for future incidents remains.

Both Sides Concede (C, C):

- Both the terrorists and the government find a middle ground, possibly involving a lesser ransom or some other form of concession.
- The hostages are released, and while both parties compromise to some degree, neither feels they've fully achieved their goals.

Strategic Implications

The Deadlock game emphasizes the consequences of firm stances, especially when the stakes involve human lives.

While standing firm can uphold principles, it can also lead to escalated dangers if neither side concedes. Introducing a third-party mediator can alter the dynamics, providing a neutral platform for communication and potentially breaking the impasse.

Conclusion

The hostage crisis in this scenario paints a grim picture of the lengths to which ideological and policy-driven stances can extend, even when lives hang in the balance. The deadlock, while understandable from the perspectives of both the terrorists and the government, underscores the dire need for channels of communication and compromise. The introduction of a third-party mediator offers a glimmer of hope, emphasizing that even in the darkest of situations, there might be a path to resolution, albeit one fraught with challenges and complexities.

Deadlock Practical Application and Analysis

Labor Union Bargains: The Deadlock Between The Automobile Company and its Union

Scenario

Tensions are high at AutoCorp, a major automobile manufacturer. The union, representing thousands of workers, believes it's time for wage hikes, citing rising living costs and past commitments.

AutoCorp, on the other hand, faces fierce market competition and believes any increase in wages could undermine its competitive position. The deadlock intensifies, and the specter of a potentially devastating strike looms large.

Game Setup

Players: AutoCorp & Union

Choices:
Concede (C)
Stand Firm (F)

Payoff Matrix (Outcomes described in terms of financial losses or gains):

	Union Concedes	**Union Stands Firm**
AutoCorp Concedes	(Minor Profit, Satisfactory Wages)	(Reduced Profit, High Wages)
AutoCorp Stands Firm	(High Profit, Unsatisfactory Wages)	(Massive Loss, Massive Loss)

Explanation of Outcomes

Both Concede (Minor Profit, Satisfactory Wages):
- Both parties decide that avoiding conflict is in their best interest.
- AutoCorp agrees to a minor wage increase, slightly affecting its profits, but ensuring production continuity.
- The union, while not getting the hike they initially demanded, ensures its members receive better compensation without resorting to strikes.

AutoCorp Concedes, Union Stands Firm (Reduced Profit, High Wages):
- AutoCorp bends to the union's demands, granting the significant wage hikes.
- The company's profit margins shrink considerably due to the increased payroll expenses.
- The union members enjoy the high wages they rallied for.

AutoCorp Stands Firm, Union Concedes (High Profit, Unsatisfactory Wages):

- The union, fearing the ramifications of a prolonged strike, withdraws its demand.
- AutoCorp retains its profit margins, not increasing wages.
- The union members continue working but at wages they deem unsatisfactory.

Both Stand Firm (Massive Loss, Massive Loss):

- Neither party is willing to budge, leading to the dreaded strike.
- Production halts, leading to huge financial losses for AutoCorp, potentially damaging its market position.
- Union members, without work, face financial hardships without wages. The prolonged conflict may also weaken the union's internal cohesion.

Strategic Implications

The game showcases the dangers of entrenched positions where mutual losses can be significant. Both parties must weigh the immediate gains of standing firm against the broader ramifications. Compromise, while not yielding the best individual outcomes, avoids the most damaging scenario where both sides suffer immensely.

Conclusion

Labor negotiations, especially involving major entities like AutoCorp and its union, aren't merely about immediate financial considerations. They embody a complex interplay of power dynamics, long-term strategies, and the human element. The Deadlock game here underscores the importance of flexibility, foresight, and the willingness to compromise, as both parties navigate the intricate dance of negotiation.

Chapter 6

Cournot Competition

"In the dance of market dynamics, the Cournot competition reminds us that players don't just react to the music, but to the moves of their fellow dancers."

Introduction

Cournot Competition, named after the French mathematician Antoine Augustin Cournot, presents a compelling analysis of oligopolistic markets.

Beyond merely providing insights into production decisions, this pivotal model offers a comprehensive understanding of the delicate balance of negotiations and strategic maneuvers within oligopolistic frameworks.

Delving into the Cournot Model's Core

The heart of Cournot's theory revolves around mutual anticipation. Within an oligopoly, firms' output decisions are predicated upon their predictions about competitors' actions. This intricate dance of mutual anticipation and response doesn't exist in isolation-it's the underpinning of myriad negotiations and strategic interactions.

Negotiations Rooted in Interdependence

The inherent interdependence of firms within

oligopolistic markets dictates that no action is without consequence. A strategic shift by one firm invariably leads to reactive or proactive adjustments by its competitors. Such dynamics set the stage for:

Harmonizing Production: Firms may enter negotiations to synchronize their output, ensuring market prices remain stable and profits are maximized.

Carving Market Niches: To mitigate direct competition, negotiations might focus on product differentiation, allowing each firm to cater to a specific market segment.

Joint Ventures and Collaborations: Recognizing shared challenges or technological advancements, firms might enter negotiations to pool resources, expertise, or capital.

Nash Equilibrium and Its Significance in Negotiations

The Nash Equilibrium, a state where firms achieve optimal outputs based on mutual anticipation, reflects the zenith of negotiation outcomes. Neither firm perceives a benefit in unilaterally deviating from this equilibrium. This mutual understanding can either be the result of tacit recognition or be solidified through explicit negotiations.

Strategic Responses and Negotiation in Market Settings

The Cournot framework illuminates the dynamic

Strategies inherent to oligopolistic markets

Collusion Dynamics: While firms might be tempted to collude, ensuring market dominance and profit maximization, such strategies often run afoul of antitrust regulations, necessitating discreet negotiations.

Market Signaling: By announcing potential shifts-like expansions or technological innovations-firms can negotiate from a position of strength, prompting rivals to recalibrate their strategies.

Continuous Re-negotiations: In dynamic markets, strategy shifts can lead to continuous renegotiations, ensuring firms remain aligned with the ever-evolving market realities.

Practical Exercises & Analysis

Understanding the Cournot competition and its negotiation dynamics benefits greatly from hands-on exercises:

Simulation Games: Participants can assume the roles of competing firms in an oligopolistic market, making production decisions based on mutual anticipation. Post-simulation analysis can focus on the decisions made, strategies adopted, and the emergence (or lack) of a Nash Equilibrium.

Case Study Analysis: Delve into real-world scenarios where firms in oligopolistic markets entered negotiations. Such analyses can highlight the external and internal pressures driving negotiations and the outcomes achieved.

Role-playing Negotiations: Simulate negotiation scenarios based on the Cournot framework, allowing participants to explore the dynamics of communication, strategic signaling, and collaboration.

Conclusion

Cournot's insights into oligopolistic markets, though conceived in the 19th century, remain a beacon for modern-day firms navigating the complex waters of negotiations and strategic decision-making.

By understanding the delicate interplay of mutual anticipation, strategic responses, and the overarching goal of achieving a Nash Equilibrium, firms can better position themselves for success in today's competitive landscape.

The lessons derived from practical exercises further solidify the Cournot model's significance, ensuring its principles are not just theoretical constructs but actionable strategies for contemporary business landscapes.

Cournot Competition Practical Application and Analysis

Market Price Settings: The Cournot Competition Between PhoneX and Mobitech

Scenario: The smartphone market is buzzing with anticipation. PhoneX and Mobitech, two industry giants, are gearing up to launch their flagship models.

With millions of customers worldwide making purchase decisions based on price and brand value, the companies' pricing strategies will determine not only individual profitability but also the market's broader dynamics.

The stakes? A potential price war, or a tacit equilibrium that guarantees healthy margins for both.

Game Setup:

Players: PhoneX & Mobitech

Choices:
High Price (H)
Medium Price (M)
Low Price (L)

Payoff Matrix (Profits in millions):

	Mobitech High	Mobitech Medium	Mobitech Low
PhoneX High	(150, 150)	(120, 160)	(90, 170)
PhoneX Medium	(160, 120)	(140, 140)	(110, 150)
PhoneX Low	(170, 90)	(150, 110)	(130, 130)

Explanation of Outcomes

Both Opt for High Price (150, 150):
- Both PhoneX and Mobitech set premium prices for their smartphones.
- The market perceives both models as high-end. While fewer units are sold due to the high price, the profit margins are significant, leading to substantial profits for both.

PhoneX High, Mobitech Medium (120, 160):
- Mobitech gains a slight edge by pricing its model slightly lower than PhoneX.
- Some potential PhoneX customers opt for Mobitech's slightly more affordable option, leading to increased profits for Mobitech and decreased profits for PhoneX.

PhoneX High, Mobitech Low (90, 170):
- Mobitech aggressively prices its phone, capturing a significant market share.

- o PhoneX, sticking to a premium pricing strategy, loses a considerable chunk of potential buyers, severely impacting its profits.

PhoneX Medium, Mobitech High (160, 120):
- o Roles reverse from the second outcome. PhoneX gains the upper hand by offering a middle-ground price, enticing customers seeking a balance between price and perceived value.

Both Opt for Medium Price (140, 140):
- o Both companies, seeking to balance market share and profitability, price their models moderately.
- o They both capture significant market segments without severely compromising on profit margins.

PhoneX Medium, Mobitech Low (110, 150):
- o Mobitech, by undercutting PhoneX, secures a larger market share, though at the cost of lower profit margins per unit.

PhoneX Low, Mobitech High (170, 90):
- o PhoneX adopts an aggressive pricing strategy, luring away potential Mobitech customers and maximizing its market share.

PhoneX Low, Mobitech Medium (150, 110):
- o While PhoneX's aggressive pricing wins over many customers, Mobitech's moderate pricing ensures it retains a loyal customer base willing to pay slightly more.

Both Opt for Low Price (130, 130):
- o A full-blown price war ensues as both companies drastically reduce prices.
- o The market is flooded with affordable high-end smartphones. While unit sales skyrocket, profit margins are thin, leading to comparable profits for both manufacturers.

Strategic Implications

The Cournot Competition framework suggests that both companies must anticipate the other's move. A miscalculation can lead to lost market share or decreased profitability.

Mutual decisions to maintain high or medium prices can ensure industry stability and healthy profits. However, the temptation to capture larger market shares with lower prices can lead to price wars, affecting the industry's overall health.

Conclusion

In the fiercely competitive smartphone market, pricing strategy is paramount. Through the Cournot Competition lens, PhoneX and Mobitech's decisions not only determine their individual fates but shape the industry's trajectory.

Their choices highlight the delicate balance between short-term gains and long-term stability in competitive markets.

Cournot Competition Practical Application and Analysis

Divorce Settlement: The Cournot Competition Between Spouses

Scenario

Love once blossomed between Taylor and Jordan, but now, as their marriage withers, they face the arduous task of dividing their joint assets.

Both spouses, armed with attorneys and fueled by emotions, aim to secure the lion's share. However, while keen to maximize their portion, each is wary of the other gaining too much - a delicate balance of self-interest and ensuring fairness.

Game Setup

Players: Taylor & Jordan

Choices:
Demand High (DH)
Demand Low (DL)

Payoff Matrix (Described in terms of the satisfaction/contentment regarding the asset division for Taylor and Jordan):

	Jordan Demands High	**Jordan Demands Low**
Taylor Demands High	Equal Division (Medium, Medium)	Taylor Gets More, Jordan Gets Less (High, Low)
Taylor Demands Low	Taylor Gets Less, Jordan Gets More (Low, High)	Amicable Division (High, High)

Explanation of Outcomes

Both Demand High (DH, DH):
- o When Taylor and Jordan both come with high demands, the result is a tense negotiation where neither party is willing to budge significantly. The assets are eventually divided somewhat equally, but neither party is entirely content with the outcome.

Taylor Demands High, Jordan Demands Low (DH, DL):
- o In this scenario, Taylor pushes for more, while Jordan, possibly wanting to avoid prolonged conflict or out of a sense of concession, settles for less. Taylor ends up with a larger share, feeling more content, whereas Jordan may harbor regrets or resentment.

Taylor Demands Low, Jordan Demands High (DL, DH):

- The roles reverse from the previous scenario. Taylor, for reasons of simplicity or fairness, lowers their demands, while Jordan pushes hard. This results in Jordan securing more assets, leading to satisfaction for Jordan and potential regret or disappointment for Taylor.

Both Demand Low (DL, DL):

- Both Taylor and Jordan, driven by a mutual desire for amicability or quick resolution, lower their demands. The division is perceived as fair and harmonious by both, and they part ways with a sense of satisfaction and closure.

Strategic Implications

The Cournot Competition emphasizes the dynamics of simultaneous decision-making where the choices of one player affect the outcomes of the other.

In a divorce setting, emotions, legal advice, and future plans can deeply influence each spouse's demands. The game presents the delicate balance between self-interest and mutual respect.

Open communication can potentially shift the game towards the more amicable "Both Demand Low" scenario, but external factors can pull it toward the other, more contentious outcomes.

Conclusion

The division of assets during a divorce, as modeled by the Cournot Competition, showcases the challenges and intricacies of reaching a satisfactory settlement.

While the game mechanics offer a structured approach to understanding potential outcomes, the human emotions and complexities involved mean that real-life scenarios can play out in unpredictable ways.

Still, the hope remains that, through understanding, compromise, and sometimes the hard lessons of negotiation, both parties can find a path to healing and new beginnings.

Chapter 7
The Centipede Game

"The Centipede Game, with its winding path and iterative choices, mirrors the journey of negotiations, reminding us that foresight and trust can transform adversaries into partners on a shared path."

Introduction

The world of game theory provides an array of fascinating models that explore the complexity of human decision-making. One such intriguing model is the Centipede Game. With its sequential structure and iterative decisions, it serves as an illustrative tool to understand the nuances of negotiations and strategic interactions.

Game Structure and Strategy

At its core, the Centipede Game is a sequential game where two players repeatedly face a decision. To continue the game and increase the potential payoff for both, or to end the game and claim a larger share of the pot for themselves.

Each decision to continue increases the overall pot but reduces the immediate payoff for the deciding player. The game ends when a player decides to take the pot, or after a predetermined number of rounds.

Strategically, the game challenges traditional notions

of rationality. A purely rational player would end the game at the first opportunity, securing the maximum immediate reward. However, if both players cooperate, there's a potential for a larger cumulative reward.

Rationality and Forward Induction

The traditional paradigm of rationality, where players optimize their immediate payoff, suggests that the Centipede Game should end immediately.

However, the game's sequential nature introduces the concept of forward induction. Players anticipate future actions and adjust their current decisions accordingly. If both players believe the other will cooperate in future turns, they might continue the game, increasing the overall payoff.

Yet, this cooperative outcome contrasts with the "rational" decision to maximize immediate gains. This disparity highlights the tension between short-term optimization and the potential benefits of forward-thinking and cooperation.

The Centipede Game offers several insights relevant to negotiations

Short-Term vs. Long-Term Rewards: Just as players must decide between immediate gains or potential future rewards, negotiators must often balance short-term concessions with long-term benefits.

Trust and Cooperation: The game underscores the importance of trust in negotiations. If one party believes the other will cooperate in future stages, they might be more willing to make concessions now.

Anticipating Future Moves: Much like forward induction, successful negotiators must anticipate future decisions, not just immediate reactions.

The Risk of Defection: Just as the Centipede Game can end abruptly with a player's decision, negotiations can break down if one party perceives too much risk or feels the other party is not negotiating in good faith.

Practical Exercises & Analysis

Playing the Centipede Game

Engage participants in actual rounds of the game. Post-game, analyze the decisions made and discuss the tension between cooperative and competitive strategies.

Negotiation Role-Playing: Create negotiation scenarios inspired by the Centipede Game. For instance, a negotiation over a business merger where both parties can make sequential concessions or demands, balancing immediate gains with the potential for a more lucrative partnership.

Comparative Analysis: Compare outcomes from traditional negotiation exercises with those from Centipede-inspired negotiations. Discuss the impact of sequential decision-making and forward induction on negotiation outcomes.

Conclusion

The Centipede Game, in its deceptive simplicity, offers profound insights into the complexity of decision-making and negotiations. It challenges conventional notions of rationality, emphasizing the importance of forward-thinking, trust, and cooperation.

For negotiators, understanding the dynamics of the Centipede Game can provide valuable strategies for navigating complex negotiations, ensuring both immediate and future benefits are taken into account.

Centipede Game Practical Application and Analysis

Partnership Agreement: The Centipede Game Between Two Business Partners

Scenario

Entrepreneurial spirit runs high in the veins of Casey and Alex, two ambitious partners keen on launching a promising startup. Their journey is marked by successive investment rounds, with each phase offering its own set of rewards and challenges.

At every juncture, they face a pressing decision: to further invest, driving their startup ahead, or to back out, pocketing the investment and leaving the venture's fate hanging. Their choices not only mirror their trust in the business but also in each other.

Game Setup

Players: Casey & Alex

Choices at each stage:
Invest (I)
Exit (E)

Game Structure

The game consists of multiple stages (let's consider four for simplicity), where each partner decides whether to invest or exit in alternating turns.

Stage 1: Casey decides.
Stage 2: Alex decides.
Stage 3: Casey decides.
Stage 4: Alex decides.

Payoff Matrix:
(For simplicity, we'll consider a linear increase in potential payoff for each stage of investment. The numbers used are illustrative.)

	Alex Invests	**Alex Exits**
Casey Invests	Move to next stage	Alex takes all; Casey gets nothing (0, High)
Casey Exits	Casey takes all; Alex gets nothing (High, 0)	Both take a moderate share (Medium, Medium)

Explanation of Outcomes

Both Invest through All Stages (I, I, I, I):
- o Casey and Alex trust each other and the potential of their startup. Their continuous investments lead to the growth of the business, maximizing long-term rewards.

One Partner Exits in an Earlier Stage:
- o If Casey or Alex decides to exit at any stage, they take the cumulative investments up to that point, leaving the other partner with nothing from the venture.
- o This can be influenced by factors like perceived risk, lack of trust in the business model, or

external opportunities luring a partner away.

Both Decide to Exit at the Same Stage (E, E):
- o   If both decide to exit at the same stage, it indicates a mutual lack of faith in the venture's future or a collective desire to cut losses and move on. Both take a moderate share, reflecting the investments made up to that point.

Strategic Implications

The Centipede Game, in the context of a partnership agreement, sheds light on the dynamics of trust and risk assessment.

A partner's choice to invest or exit is a strong indicator of their belief in the startup's success and their trust in their co-partner.

Exiting early might seem like a safe option to secure immediate gains, but staying in the game can lead to more significant rewards. This requires a clear assessment of business potential and partner intentions.

Open communication and aligned vision can lead partners to invest through all stages, maximizing the potential for success.

Conclusion

Embarking on a startup journey, as depicted by the Centipede Game, illuminates the complexities of trust, strategy, and risk that business partners face. Each decision point, marked by the choice to invest further or to exit, becomes a testament to their belief in their shared dream. Whether they walk this journey side by side till the end or part ways earlier, their choices reverberate through the annals of their entrepreneurial story.

Centipede Game Practical Application and Analysis

Real Estate Dealings: The Centipede Game Between Buyer A and Seller B

Scenario

The metropolitan cityscape serves as the backdrop for an intense real estate negotiation. Buyer A, seeking a prime piece of property for future ventures, sits across from Seller B, who's looking to capitalize on this high-demand asset. Round after round, the property's price is on an upward trajectory. But with each increase, both parties face the dilemma: continue to the next round, hoping for a better deal, or end negotiations and finalize the purchase?

Game Setup

Players: Buyer A & Seller B

Rounds: Multiple rounds of negotiation (for simplicity, we'll consider 5 rounds).

Choices in each round:
Continue (C)
Finalize (F)

Payoff Matrix (Described in terms of potential profits/losses for Buyer A and Seller B in each round):

Round/Decision	Buyer A Continues	Buyer A Finalizes
1 (Seller B)	Round 2	($90k, $110k)
2 (Buyer A)	Round 3	($85k, $115k)
3 (Seller B)	Round 4	($80k, $120k)
4 (Buyer A)	Round 5	($75k, $125k)
5 (Seller B)	End (No Deal)	($70k, $130k)

(Note: The monetary values in the matrix are arbitrary and represent potential profits/losses. For instance, in Round 1, if Buyer A finalizes, they might secure the property for $90k, whereas Seller B secures a sale price of $110k.)

Explanation of Outcomes

Round 1:
- o Seller B can decide to raise the price and proceed to Round 2, or accept a deal at $110k.
- o Buyer A, if deciding to finalize here, would purchase the property for $90k.

Round 2:
- o Buyer A can choose to accept the raised price or push for another round, hoping Seller B might offer better terms.
- o Seller B, if the deal finalizes here, sells the

property for $115k.

Round 3:
- o Seller B now faces the decision again. Prices go higher, but so does the risk of Buyer A walking away from the deal.
- o Buyer A, opting to finalize, acquires the property for $80k.

Round 4:
- o Buyer A can attempt one last push, hoping for the best possible terms in the final round.
- o Seller B, if securing a deal here, receives $125k for the property.

Round 5:
- o This is the final round. If Seller B continues, there's no deal - both parties have reached their limits.
- o If Buyer A chooses to finalize, the purchase is made at the steepest price of $70k, with Seller B reaping a sale price of $130k.

Strategic Implications

The Centipede Game, applied to this real estate scenario, emphasizes the tug-of-war between immediate gains and potential future benefits.

Each player must evaluate the other's determination and willingness to proceed or end the negotiations. The risk grows with each round: while potential profits increase, so does the possibility of walking away with nothing.

Conclusion

Real estate dealings, especially in high-demand areas, are fraught with strategic decisions and a balancing act of risks and rewards. The Centipede Game, as exemplified by Buyer A and Seller B's interactions, underlines the sequential nature of such negotiations.

Each move can lead to better terms or the end of discussions. It's a dance of strategy, intuition, and evaluating one's position at every step, ensuring the quest for the best deal doesn't result in a missed opportunity.

Chapter 8

The Traveler's Dilemma

"In the journey of choices, the Traveler's Dilemma illuminates the fine line between intuition and logic, teaching negotiators that sometimes the path less rational may lead to the most rewarding destinations."

Introduction

Within the realm of game theory, certain models stand out not just for their mathematical intrigue but for their profound reflections on human behavior. One such paradigmatic example is the Traveler's Dilemma, a non-zero-sum game that illustrates the paradoxes of rationality and offers significant insights into the dynamics of negotiations.

The Game and its Paradox

The Traveler's Dilemma involves two travelers who, having bought identical items, find them damaged during their journey. The airline offers compensation, but there's a catch. Without knowing the item's price, the airline asks each traveler to independently quote a price. If both quote the same price, that's what they'll be compensated.

However, if one quotes a lower price, he gets a small bonus, while the other traveler, quoting the higher price, is penalized. The dilemma? Rationality dictates both should quote the minimum possible to ensure a bonus, but this leads to a suboptimal outcome for both.

This game, at its heart, showcases the paradox of rational decision-making. Logic would have each player undercut the other continually, leading to the lowest possible payout-a seemingly irrational outcome when larger, mutual gains could be had.

Rationality vs. Intuition

Central to the Traveler's Dilemma is the tension between rational, analytical decision-making and intuitive, cooperative strategies. While mathematical rationality suggests that undercutting is the logical strategy, human intuition often guides players towards a higher, cooperative quote, maximizing mutual benefits.

In negotiations, this tension is omnipresent. Parties often face the choice between immediate, self-serving gains and longer-term, mutual benefits. The Traveler's Dilemma serves as a metaphorical reminder that pure rationality might not always lead to the best outcomes in negotiations.

The dynamics of the Traveler's Dilemma play out in real-world price negotiations

Bidding Wars: Similar to the travelers undercutting each other, bidders in auctions can drive prices down, sometimes even incurring losses to outbid competitors.

Price Matching Policies: Retailers often promise to match or beat competitors' prices, leading to a race to the bottom where both sellers might end up with diminished profits.

Contract Negotiations: In contract bids, companies may undercut to win contracts but might compromise on quality or even face losses, reminiscent of the paradox faced by the travelers.

Practical Exercises & Analysis

Traveler's Dilemma Simulation

Participants can engage in several rounds of the game, with varying bonus/penalty values. Analyzing the outcomes can offer insights into decision-making patterns and the tension between rationality and intuition.

Role-playing Price Negotiations: Simulate real-world scenarios, like contract bids or retail price wars, drawing parallels with the Traveler's Dilemma. Debrief sessions can discuss strategies, outcomes, and alternative negotiation tactics.

Historical Case Studies: Analyze real-world price wars or bidding scenarios that mirror the Traveler's Dilemma. Dissecting these cases can offer valuable lessons on the pitfalls of purely rational strategies and the potential benefits of cooperative negotiations.

Conclusion

The Traveler's Dilemma, while a simple game in

structure, offers profound insights into the complexities of human decision-making, especially in the context of negotiations.

It underscores the limitations of pure rationality, emphasizing the value of intuition, cooperation, and long-term thinking. For negotiators, understanding the essence of this game provides a framework to navigate the intricate balance between self-interest and mutual benefit, ensuring negotiations lead to outcomes that are both optimal and sustainable.

Traveler's Dilemma Practical Application and Analysis

Estate Distribution: The Traveler's Dilemma Between Siblings

Scenario

After the passing of a family patriarch, an expansive estate awaits distribution among two siblings, Chris and Jamie.

Their father's wish was for them to decide on the distribution amicably. Now, they're faced with a moral and financial quandary. They can either demand a larger portion of the estate, driven by individual interest, or opt for a fair and equitable split, honoring their father's memory.

But if both get entangled in greed, disputes will ensue, casting a shadow on their relationship and delaying the inheritance process.

Game Setup

Players: Chris & Jamie

Choices:
Claim Larger Portion (L)
Settle for Equitable Share (E)

Payoff Matrix (Described in terms of satisfaction/contentment regarding the asset distribution for Chris and Jamie):

	Jamie Claims Larger	Jamie Settles Equitably
Chris Claims Larger	Disputes & Delays (Low, Low)	Chris Gets More, Jamie Less (High, Low)
Chris Settles Equitably	Jamie Gets More, Chris Less (Low, High)	Amicable Division (High, High)

Explanation of Outcomes

Both Claim Larger Portion (L, L):
- o Both Chris and Jamie, driven by self-interest, claim a larger share of the estate.
- o This results in conflicts, potentially leading to legal disputes, tarnishing family ties, and delaying the distribution process. Neither sibling is content with this outcome.

Chris Claims Larger, Jamie Settles Equitably (L, E):
- o Chris, driven by individual desires, claims more of the inheritance, while Jamie, either out of respect for their father's wishes or wanting to avoid conflict, settles for a smaller share.
- o Chris ends up with a more significant portion and is satisfied, but Jamie may feel slighted or exploited.

Chris Settles Equitably, Jamie Claims Larger (E, L):

- o Jamie seeks a larger share, while Chris, driven by a sense of fairness or avoiding disputes, agrees to an equitable division.
- o This results in Jamie getting more, leading to satisfaction for Jamie but potential feelings of regret or being undervalued for Chris.

Both Settle Equitably (E, E):

- o Both Chris and Jamie prioritize family ties, mutual respect, and their father's wishes over personal gain.
- o They settle for an equitable distribution, leading to mutual satisfaction and a strengthening of their bond.

Strategic Implications

The Traveler's Dilemma, in the context of estate distribution, reflects the internal tug-of-war between individual gain and collective harmony.

Family dynamics, past experiences, and personal financial situations can influence decisions.

Open communication, understanding each other's perspectives, and possibly seeking mediation can help navigate this dilemma effectively.

Conclusion

Estate distribution, as depicted through the lens of the Traveler's Dilemma, delves deep into the complexities of human nature, familial bonds, and the allure of material wealth. As Chris and Jamie stand at this crossroads, their choices become a reflection of their values, priorities, and the legacy they wish to carry forward.

Whether driven by individual aspirations or collective respect, their decisions will resonate through the annals of their family history, serving as a testament to the intricate interplay of emotion, morality, and desire.

Traveler's Dilemma Practical Application and Analysis

Car Purchases: The Traveler's Dilemma Between Jane and the Car Dealer

Scenario

At EliteCars showroom, Jane has her eyes set on a sleek sedan. The dealer, Mr. Smith, has some room to provide a discount, though he hopes Jane is oblivious to this fact. Jane, having heard rumors of discounts, considers playing coy, believing this might lead Mr. Smith to offer an even sweeter deal to close the sale. Both stand on a decision precipice: to reveal or conceal their cards?

Game Setup

Players: Jane & Mr. Smith (the dealer)

Choices:
Reveal (R)
Conceal (C)

Payoff Matrix (Outcomes described in terms of financial loss or gain for Jane and the dealer):

	Dealer Reveals	Dealer Conceals
Jane Reveals	(Standard Discount, Moderate Profit)	(Small Discount, High Profit)
Jane Conceals	(Big Discount, Low Profit)	(No Discount, Maximum Profit)

Explanation of Outcomes

Both Reveal (Standard Discount, Moderate Profit):
- o Jane mentions the rumored discount upfront. Mr. Smith, appreciating her straightforwardness, offers the standard discount.
- o Jane secures a decent deal, and Mr. Smith makes a moderate profit from the sale.

Jane Reveals, Dealer Conceals (Small Discount, High Profit):
- o Jane brings up the discount, but Mr. Smith, feigning ignorance, offers a minimal reduction in price, suggesting it's the best he can do.
- o Jane gets only a tiny discount, while Mr. Smith pockets a higher profit.

Jane Conceals, Dealer Reveals (Big Discount, Low Profit):
- o Jane acts unaware of any discounts. To entice her to close the deal, Mr. Smith voluntarily

offers a larger-than-usual discount.
- o Jane benefits from a significant price reduction, while Mr. Smith's profit margin diminishes.

Both Conceal (No Discount, Maximum Profit):
- o Jane doesn't mention any discount, and Mr. Smith plays along, offering the car at its full price.
- o Jane misses out on any potential savings, and Mr. Smith enjoys the maximum profit from the sale.

Strategic Implications

The game revolves around the balance of information and intuition. While revealing knowledge can lead to a guaranteed, albeit standard outcome, concealing intentions might lead to the best or worst financial results.

Trust and perceived intentions play crucial roles. Jane must judge if Mr. Smith will offer a better deal if she feigns ignorance. Conversely, Mr. Smith must decide if offering a spontaneous discount will clinch the sale.

Conclusion

The intricacies of the Traveler's Dilemma, when set in the context of a car purchase, underscore the delicate dance of negotiation, information asymmetry, and human intuition.

Both Jane and Mr. Smith, in their quest to secure the best deal, must navigate their decisions based not only on what they know but also on what they believe the other party might do. The outcome of their interaction provides a fascinating exploration of strategy, psychology, and the ever-present desire to "win" in a negotiation.

Chapter 9

The Battle of the Sexes

"In the dance of negotiation, the Battle of the Sexes illustrates that understanding isn't just about compromise but harmonizing distinct rhythms to create a melody of mutual benefit."

Introduction

In the realm of game theory, few models are as engaging as the Battle of the Sexes. This game, often presented humorously as a couple deciding between two events, transcends its playful veneer to provide a profound exploration of coordination, communication, and negotiation dynamics.

Particularly, when placed in the context of gender and workplace negotiations, the game offers a myriad of insights.

Game Framework

The Battle of the Sexes is essentially a coordination game. In its traditional representation, it involves two players (often depicted as a couple) who have to decide independently on attending one of two events-say, a ballet or a football game.

Each player has a preference; however, both prefer attending the same event over attending different events. The dilemma arises because their primary preferences are misaligned, yet there's a mutual benefit in coordinating their choices.

The game presents multiple equilibria

Both attending the ballet, both attending the football game, or a mixed strategy where choices are unpredictable. The challenge lies in coordinating to achieve mutual benefit.

Coordination and Communication

Central to the Battle of the Sexes is the theme of coordination. When players can't communicate, they might fail to coordinate, leading to suboptimal outcomes. However, with effective communication, they can negotiate a solution that, while it might favor one party's preference, is mutually beneficial as they end up attending the same event.

The game underscores the significance of communication in negotiations

Sometimes, achieving a mutually beneficial outcome might involve conceding primary preferences. Yet, without open dialogue, even secondary preferences (like attending the same event) might be unattainable.

Implications in Gender and Workplace Negotiations

The implications of the Battle of the Sexes extend far beyond couples deciding on events. In the context of gender dynamics and workplace negotiations: Gender Preferences: Historically, gender roles and societal expectations have created distinct preferences in workplace settings. These differences can lead to misaligned priorities, reminiscent of the Battle of the Sexes.

Achieving Consensus: Just as the couple seeks to attend the same event, workplace teams aim for consensus. Despite differing primary goals, the shared objective is a coordinated, harmonious decision.

Power Dynamics: Often, in gender and workplace negotiations, power dynamics play a pivotal role. The Battle of the Sexes highlights how, in the absence of balanced power, one party's preferences might dominate, leading to skewed negotiation outcomes.

Practical Exercises & Analysis

Role-Playing the Game: Participants can assume roles and engage in multiple rounds of the game, with varied preferences and power dynamics. Analyzing outcomes can reveal patterns in decision-making and the role of communication.

Workplace Simulation: Create scenarios where teams must make decisions with misaligned priorities, mirroring the Battle of the Sexes. Post-decision analysis can delve into negotiation strategies, communication effectiveness, and the influence of power dynamics.

Case Studies: Evaluate real-world workplace negotiations, especially those with evident gender dynamics. Dissecting these cases can offer insights into effective and ineffective negotiation strategies and the significance of open communication.

Conclusion

The Battle of the Sexes, while conceptually simple, serves as a lens through which the intricacies of negotiation can be viewed, especially in contexts rife with power dynamics and misaligned priorities. It emphasizes the paramount importance of open communication and the often-underestimated value of secondary preferences in achieving coordinated, mutually beneficial outcomes.

For modern workplaces and in understanding gender dynamics, the game is a timely reminder of the complexities and potential harmonies of decision-making processes.

Battle of the Sexes Practical Application and Analysis

Corporate Sale: The Battle of the Sexes Between Company X and Company Y

Scenario

The business world is abuzz with the news: Company X, a market veteran with a strong brand reputation, is being acquired by Company Y, an emerging force with its distinct brand identity.

The acquisition promises potential synergies, but a looming question remains: Which brand name should they continue under post-acquisition? While both companies have a preference for their original brand names, they understand the importance of presenting a unified brand image in the market.

Game Setup

Players: Company X & Company Y

Choices:
Retain Own Brand (Own)
Adopt Other's Brand (Other)

Payoff Matrix (Described in terms of satisfaction/contentment regarding the brand choice for Company X and Company Y):

	Company Y Chooses Own	Company Y Chooses Other
Company X Chooses Own	Brand Conflict (Low, Low)	Company X Dominates (High, Medium)
Company X Chooses Other	Company Y Dominates (Medium, High)	Unified Branding (High, High)

Explanation of Outcomes

Both Choose Their Own Brand (Own, Own):
- o Company X and Company Y, driven by pride and belief in their respective brand values, both choose to retain their original brand names.
- o This leads to internal brand conflict, market confusion, and reduced synergistic benefits. Both companies find this outcome less than optimal.

Company X Chooses Own, Company Y Chooses Other (Own, Other):
- o Company X sticks with its established brand, while Company Y, recognizing the value or legacy of Company X's brand, chooses to adopt it.
- o Company X experiences high satisfaction due to its brand dominance, while Company Y has medium satisfaction, deriving some benefits

from the established brand but having to let go of its original identity.

Company X Chooses Other, Company Y Chooses Own (Other, Own):

- o Company X, seeing potential in Company Y's brand or wanting a fresh start, decides to adopt Company Y's brand. Meanwhile, Company Y prefers its brand.
- o Company Y feels a sense of triumph with its brand dominating, leading to high satisfaction. Company X, having made a strategic decision, has medium satisfaction.

Both Choose the Other's Brand (Other, Other):

- o Ironically, both companies, in an attempt to show willingness for change or integration, choose the other's brand.
- o This outcome results in mutual appreciation and recognition of each other's value, leading to high satisfaction for both, but it might necessitate a further discussion to decide on the final brand.

Strategic Implications

The Battle of the Sexes, when applied to corporate branding decisions, highlights the importance of communication, mutual respect, and strategic foresight.

While individual brand preferences can be strong, the shared objective should be maximizing post-acquisition synergies and market perception. External factors, such as market research or customer feedback, can provide invaluable insights to guide this decision.

Conclusion

As Company X and Company Y embark on their merged journey, the brand they choose becomes symbolic of their collective vision, values, and market promise.

The Battle of the Sexes game, in this context, serves as a reminder of the challenges and opportunities that arise when two entities, each with its identity, come together. The choices made will not only shape their market positioning but also the internal culture and ethos of the newly merged entity.

It's a dance of strategy, ego, and compromise, culminating in a decision that will pave their way forward in the business world.

Battle of the Sexes Practical Application and Analysis

Trade Agreements: The Battle of the Sexes Between Agroland and Industrica

Scenario

In the grand hall of international diplomacy, representatives from Agroland and Industrica sit down for a pivotal negotiation. Agroland, with its vast fertile lands, seeks favorable terms to export its agricultural bounty.

Industrica, known for its factories and technological prowess, wants its manufactured goods to find prime markets in Agroland. The goal? A trade agreement that uplifts both nations. But which sector will gain prominence in the deal?

Game Setup

Players: Agroland & Industrica

Choices:
Prioritize Agriculture (A)
Prioritize Manufacturing (M)

Payoff Matrix (Outcomes described in terms of trade benefits):

	Industrica Prioritizes Agriculture	Industrica Prioritizes Manufacturing
Agroland Prioritizes Agriculture	(Moderate, Moderate)	(High, Low)
Agroland Prioritizes Manufacturing	(Low, High)	(Balanced, Balanced)

Explanation of Outcomes

Both Prioritize Agriculture (Moderate, Moderate):
- o Both nations focus on promoting agricultural trade.
- o Agroland gets a reasonable deal for its products, but since both parties are aligned on the same sector, neither country enjoys the full benefits of diversified trade.
- o The trade leans heavily on agricultural products with few manufactured goods in the mix, leading to moderate benefits for both.
- o Agroland Prioritizes Agriculture, Industrica

Prioritizes Manufacturing (High, Low):
- o Agroland manages to strike an excellent deal for its agricultural exports, while also agreeing to import Industrica's manufactured goods.
- o Industrica benefits less because while its

manufactured goods find a market in Agroland, it has to make significant concessions on agricultural imports.

Agroland Prioritizes Manufacturing, Industrica Prioritizes Agriculture (Low, High):

- o The tables turn. Industrica secures a favorable deal for its agricultural imports while ensuring a market for Agroland's manufactured products.
- o Agroland, though gaining a market for its manufactured goods, has to make significant agricultural concessions, benefiting less from the deal.

Both Prioritize Manufacturing (Balanced, Balanced):

- o Both nations decide to prioritize manufacturing in their trade agreement.

- o A diverse mix of goods flows between the countries: Agroland imports technological and manufactured products, and Industrica brings in a limited but valuable range of agricultural products.
- o The balanced focus ensures that both nations derive equitable benefits from the trade, promoting economic growth and fostering diplomatic ties.

Strategic Implications

Mutual understanding and compromise are key. If both nations rigidly stick to promoting only one sector, they risk losing out on the broad benefits of diversified trade.

The Battle of the Sexes game highlights the importance of alignment and the potential pitfalls of misaligned priorities in negotiations.

Conclusion

Trade negotiations between nations, as epitomized by Agroland and Industrica, are intricate affairs that go beyond mere numbers and tariffs. The Battle of the Sexes game, applied to this scenario, showcases the balance of national priorities, mutual benefits, and the art of compromise.

As nations tread the delicate path of international diplomacy and trade, their choices not only shape economic outcomes but also sculpt the very nature of international relations.

Chapter 10

The Dictator Game

"In the arena of negotiations, the Dictator Game stands as a mirror, reflecting not just our strategies but our inherent altruism, reminding us that true power lies in benevolence."

Introduction

In the vast landscape of game theory, The Dictator Game emerges as a compelling exploration of human altruism and fairness. Unlike other games that focus on mutual benefit or competitive advantage, The Dictator Game delves into the unilateral power of decision-making and its implications.

When this game is juxtaposed with the context of negotiations, it reveals profound insights into how notions of fairness and altruism shape decision-making processes.

Understanding Altruism and Fairness

The Dictator Game is straightforward in its setup: one player, the "dictator," is given a sum of money and has the power to offer any portion of it, even none, to the second player.

The second player, passive in this setup, must accept whatever amount is given. The game, at its core, is a study of altruism. The dictator, devoid of any external pressures or reciprocity threats, chooses how much to give purely based on their intrinsic sense of fairness or altruism.

Results and Interpretations

While traditional economic theories suggest that individuals act out of self-interest, results from numerous iterations of The Dictator Game often defy this assumption. Many dictators choose to give away a portion of their endowment, suggesting an inherent tendency towards fairness or altruism.

However, interpretations vary. Some see it as a reflection of social norms, where giving is seen positively. Others interpret it as an aversion to inequality. There's also a view that, in some contexts, the dictator gives to enhance their self-image or due to the psychological benefits of being seen as generous.

How Fairness Influences Negotiations

Perceived Fairness: In negotiations, perceived fairness often plays a more significant role than objective outcomes. Parties are more likely to accept deals they perceive as fair, even if they are not objectively optimal.

Building Trust: Demonstrations of fairness or altruism, as seen in The Dictator Game, can foster trust. In negotiations, trust can pave the way for more open discussions and mutually beneficial outcomes.

Reputation and Future Interactions: Just as a dictator's choice might be influenced by how they wish to be perceived, negotiators are often influenced by considerations of future interactions and their reputation.

Psychological Well-being: Fairness in negotiations isn't just about equitable outcomes. It's also linked to the psychological well-being of the negotiators, affecting their satisfaction levels and commitment to the negotiated agreement.

Practical Exercises & Analysis

Role-Playing The Dictator Game: Engage participants in The Dictator Game, and post-game, discuss the motivations behind their decisions. This exercise can shed light on individual perceptions of fairness and altruism.

Negotiation Simulations with Unequal Power Dynamics: Model negotiations where one party has significantly more power, mirroring the dictator's position. Analyze how this power is used, whether altruistically, fairly, or self-servingly.

Case Studies: Explore real-world negotiations where one party had overwhelming power. Analyze their decisions, outcomes, and the role of fairness in shaping these outcomes.

Conclusion

The Dictator Game, in its elegance and simplicity, serves as a profound exploration of human nature, particularly our inclinations towards fairness and altruism. In the world of negotiations, where power dynamics, reputations, and future interactions play pivotal roles, understanding the nuances of The Dictator Game offers negotiators invaluable insights.

It serves as a reminder that beyond numbers and objective outcomes, the human elements of trust, fairness, and altruism remain at the heart of every negotiation.

The Dictator Game Practical Application and Analysis

Mortgage Foreclosure: The Dictator Game Between The Bank and The Homeowner

Scenario

Amid economic upheaval, countless dreams hang in the balance. Among them is the homeowner's dream of retaining their cherished residence. The bank, holding the mortgage, finds itself in a position of power.

The homeowner, grappling with financial constraints, is desperate for a loan modification to prevent foreclosure. The decision lies solely with the bank, with the homeowner fervently hoping for a display of compassion and understanding.

Game Setup

Players: The Bank & The Homeowner

Choices for the Bank:
Foreclose (F)
Grant Loan Modification (M)

Note: In the Dictator Game, one player (in this case, the Bank) has the power to make a unilateral decision, while the other player (the Homeowner) has no strategic move but can only accept the outcome.

Potential Outcomes

Bank Chooses to Foreclose (F):
- The bank, driven by its financial interests or a risk-averse policy, decides to foreclose on the property.
- Implications for the Bank: The bank might recover a significant portion of its loan by selling the foreclosed property. However, this could tarnish its reputation, affecting customer trust and loyalty in the long run.
- Implications for the Homeowner: The homeowner loses the property, leading to emotional distress, potential homelessness, and a hit to their credit score.

Bank Grants Loan Modification (M):
- The bank, considering the homeowner's situation and potential long-term relations or its public image, offers a loan modification. This can involve reduced interest rates, extended loan tenure, or other amicable terms.

Implications for the Bank

By doing this, the bank might experience a short-term financial setback. However, this act can boost its reputation, depicting it as a compassionate institution, and may lead to increased customer loyalty and positive word of mouth.

Implications for the Homeowner

The homeowner gets a reprieve, allowing them to retain their property and offering them a chance to stabilize their financial situation.

Strategic Implications

The Dictator Game, when framed within the context of mortgage foreclosure, underscores the power dynamics between financial institutions and individual borrowers.

While the bank holds the reins, its decisions can significantly influence its public perception and long-term customer relationships.

External factors, such as government regulations, public sentiment, and economic trends, can weigh on the bank's decision.

Conclusion

The delicate dance between the bank and the homeowner in the Dictator Game provides a stark glimpse into the realities faced by many during economic downturns.

With the power of decision vested entirely in the bank, the homeowner's fate hangs precariously. However, the bank's choice, be it driven by sheer economics or laced with empathy, will reverberate beyond just financial implications.

It shapes narratives, molds public opinion, and, most crucially, impacts lives. In this game of power and vulnerability, the stakes are real, and the outcomes, profoundly consequential.

The Dictator Game Practical Application and Analysis

Salary Negotiations: The Dictator Game Between John and the HR Manager

Scenario

John, renowned in the tech industry for his software development prowess, is sitting across the table from Ms. Parker, the HR manager of TechTitan Inc. The stakes are high.

Ms. Parker holds all the cards: she can offer John a competitive salary befitting his skills or go for a lower package, aiming to save costs for TechTitan. But if she pushes too low, John might walk, and the company will miss out on a top-tier talent.

Game Setup

Players: John & Ms. Parker (the HR manager)

Choices for Ms. Parker:
Competitive Package (CP)
Lowball Offer (LO)

Outcome Matrix (Outcomes described in terms of job satisfaction for John and financial implications for TechTitan):

	Ms. Parker offers CP	**Ms. Parker offers LO**
John's Response	Accepts (High Satisfaction, Standard Cost)	Rejects (No Job, Maximum Savings)

(Note: In the Dictator Game, typically one player (the dictator) determines an allocation of some endowment, like money. The second player has no strategic move. In this adapted version, John has a passive role, where his action is determined by Ms. Parker's decision.)

Explanation of Outcomes

Ms. Parker offers Competitive Package:
- o Recognizing John's expertise and the value he brings, Ms. Parker proposes a salary that matches industry standards for top-tier developers.

John Accepts (High Satisfaction, Standard Cost):
- o John, feeling valued and fairly compensated, accepts the offer. He begins his role at TechTitan with high motivation and job satisfaction.
- o TechTitan incurs the standard cost for a top-tier developer but secures a valuable asset in

John.

Ms. Parker offers Lowball Offer:
- o Ms. Parker, aiming to save costs, offers a salary below what someone of John's caliber might expect.

John Rejects (No Job, Maximum Savings):
- o Feeling undervalued and knowing his worth in the market, John declines the offer, continuing his job search elsewhere.
- o TechTitan saves on payroll but misses out on hiring a top-tier developer, potentially impacting project outcomes and future revenue.

Strategic Implications

Ms. Parker's decision hinges on how TechTitan values long-term gains versus short-term savings. While saving on payroll might seem advantageous now, missing out on top talent can have cascading negative effects in terms of product quality, team morale, and company reputation.

The Dictator Game emphasizes the power dynamic in this situation. Ms. Parker has the primary decision-making power, but the consequences of her decision are felt by both players and, by extension, the wider company.

Conclusion

Salary negotiations, especially for top-tier talent, present a challenging balancing act for companies.

The Dictator Game, as applied to John and Ms. Parker's situation, showcases the profound effects of unilateral decision-making. While Ms. Parker has the immediate power, the ripple effects of her choice will shape John's career trajectory and TechTitan's future.

It's a reminder of the responsibility that comes with power, especially in the nuanced world of HR and talent acquisition.

Chapter 11

The Peace-War Game

"In the global theater of diplomacy, the Peace-War
Game unveils the intricate dance of nations, where
everymove echoes with intentions and
implications,and the quest for harmony is a
negotiationin itself."

Introduction

Amidst the multifaceted dimensions of game theory,
the Peace-War Game offers a remarkable examination
of strategic interactions on the global stage.

As nations grapple with decisions of peace and
conflict, the game offers a lens through which the
intricate dance of international negotiations can be
better understood, revealing nuances about
diplomacy, strategy, and the very nature of human
conflict and cooperation.

Game Setup and Dynamics

The Peace-War Game is a two-player game that
mimics the choices nations face regarding cooperation
or conflict. Each player chooses between "peace" or
"war."

If both players choose peace, they both receive a
moderate reward, symbolizing the mutual benefits of
cooperation. If both opt for war, they incur a
significant cost, representing the destructive nature of
conflict. However, if one chooses peace and the other

war, the war-declaring nation secures a significant reward, capitalizing on the other's pacifism, while the peaceful nation incurs a cost.

The game encapsulates the perennial tension between trust and betrayal, cooperation and dominance.

Strategy and Diplomacy Insights

Distrust and Defensive Actions: If nations distrust each other's intentions, they might opt for war to pre-emptively protect their interests, leading to mutually detrimental outcomes.

The Value of Communication: The game underscores the significance of communication in preventing misunderstandings and building trust, thereby avoiding suboptimal outcomes.

The Temptation of Dominance: The potential gains from declaring war when another nation chooses peace represent the allure of dominance, revealing the strategic considerations nations grapple with when engaging on the international stage.

Applications in International Negotiations

Deterrence and Diplomacy: Nations often employ deterrence strategies, showcasing their willingness to engage in conflict if provoked. Yet, simultaneous diplomatic overtures aim to secure peaceful resolutions.

Coalitions and Alliances: Nations form alliances to present a united front, akin to mutual decisions for "peace" or "war" in the game, ensuring collective benefits or deterring adversaries.

Trade Negotiations: The game's principles also apply to economic contexts. In trade negotiations, nations can either cooperate, leading to mutual economic gains, or engage in trade wars, leading to potential losses for both.

Practical Exercises & Analysis

Simulating the Peace-War Game

Participants can role-play as nation leaders, making decisions based on given scenarios. Analyzing the outcomes can reveal insights into strategy formulation and the role of trust.

Case Study Evaluation

Analyze historical instances where nations faced decisions akin to the Peace-War Game, such as the Cold War dynamics between the USA and USSR, or more recent trade negotiations.

Role-playing International Summits

Simulate international negotiation scenarios where participants must navigate the dynamics of the Peace-War Game, incorporating elements like espionage, misinformation, and back-channel communications.

Conclusion

The Peace-War Game, while a structured

representation, captures the essence of the challenges, temptations, and potential rewards nations face in the intricate ballet of international negotiations.

It serves as a stark reminder that while the allure of short-term gains or dominance might be tempting, the path of communication, trust, and cooperation often holds the promise of longer-term, mutual benefits.

In the ever-evolving dance of diplomacy, understanding the tenets of the Peace-War Game equips leaders and negotiators with the insights needed to navigate the complexities of the international arena.

Peace-War Practical Application and Analysis

Diplomatic Talks: The Peace-War Game Between Northlandia and Southlandia

Scenario

Two neighboring nations, Northlandia and Southlandia, find themselves at a crossroads over the shared river that forms their border. The river, vital for both agriculture and daily needs, has seen diminished flow rates in recent years.

Each nation now faces a decision: cooperate and devise a mutual plan for the river's sustainable use, or hoard its waters unilaterally, risking conflict and heightened tensions.

Game Setup:

Players: Northlandia & Southlandia

Choices:
Cooperate (C)
Hoard (H)

Payoff Matrix:

	Southlandia Cooperates	Southlandia Hoards
Northlandia Cooperates	(Sustainable Benefit, Sustainable Benefit)	(Water Shortage, Temporary Gain)
Northlandia Hoards	(Temporary Gain, Water Shortage)	(Conflict, Conflict)

Explanation of Outcomes

Both Cooperate (Sustainable Benefit, Sustainable Benefit):

- o Both countries work together to manage the river's water, ensuring its long-term sustainability.
- o This cooperation fosters trust, which can extend to other areas of bilateral relations, boosting trade, tourism, and overall diplomatic relations.
- o Both nations enjoy uninterrupted water supply, benefiting agriculture and daily life.

Northlandia Cooperates, Southlandia Hoards (Water Shortage, Temporary Gain):

- o Northlandia faces a water shortage due to Southlandia taking more than its fair share.
- o Southlandia enjoys a temporary boost in water availability, but this short-term gain sows distrust and tension, potentially harming future interactions and trade.
- o The likelihood of Northlandia seeking international mediation or retaliating in other

areas increases.

Northlandia Hoards, Southlandia Cooperates (Temporary Gain, Water Shortage):

- o Roles are reversed from the second scenario.
- o Southlandia faces the brunt of Northlandia's unilateral decision, which, while offering Northlandia a temporary advantage, strains diplomatic ties.

Both Hoard (Conflict, Conflict):

- o Both countries, by deciding to act unilaterally, escalate the situation, leading to severe water shortages on both sides.
- o This mutual decision likely results in heightened military presence at the border, international condemnation, and the possibility of conflict.
- o Trade, diplomatic ties, and regional stability all suffer as a result.

Strategic Implications

Mutual cooperation offers the best long-term outcome for both nations. Yet, the temptation or fear of the other nation hoarding might drive one or both towards unilateral actions.

The shadow of the future plays a role here; if both nations anticipate future interactions and value long-term benefits, they'll be more inclined to cooperate.

Conclusion

The Peace-War Game, when applied to the

Northlandia-Southlandia scenario, underscores the profound impact of individual decisions on collective outcomes. While mutual cooperation holds the key to sustainable success, distrust or short-term thinking can lead to outcomes detrimental to both.

The fate of the shared river, and by extension the relations between Northlandia and Southlandia, hangs in the balance, determined by their choices in this intricate game of diplomacy and strategy.

Peace-War Practical Application and Analysis

Politics: The Peace-War Game Between Democracia and Republica

Scenario

Two neighboring nations, Democracia and Republica, have shared a historically volatile border. With rising nationalistic sentiments in both countries, they are at a crossroads: forge a lasting peace treaty or escalate into conflict. A third entity, the International Peace Organization (IPO), seeks to mediate and facilitate peaceful negotiations.

Players:
- Democracia - A democratic nation with a robust economy, aiming to maintain its trade routes.
- Republica - A republic keen on expanding its territorial boundaries for strategic advantage.
- IPO - An international body with a vested interest in regional stability.

Options

Democracia:
- Extend a peace treaty with favorable terms.
- Maintain status quo (neither peace nor war).
- Fortify border defenses, signaling potential aggression.

Republica:
- o Accept the peace treaty and reciprocate with favorable terms.
- o Maintain status quo.
- o Mobilize troops towards the border, signaling potential aggression.

IPO:
- o Propose a neutral peace treaty for both nations.
- o Impose sanctions on the aggressor.
- o Send peacekeeping forces to de-escalate tensions.

Possible Outcomes

Mutual Cooperation: Democracia extends a peace treaty, and Republica reciprocates. Result: Peaceful coexistence, economic and cultural exchange.

One-Sided Aggression: Democracia fortifies its border, while Republica maintains the status quo or

Vice Versa. Result: Tensions rise, but outright conflict is avoided. IPO might intervene to mediate.

Mutual Aggression: Both Democracia and Republica mobilize troops or fortify borders. Result: High possibility of conflict. IPO sends peacekeeping forces and imposes sanctions on both nations. Peace through Mediation: IPO proposes a neutral treaty. Democracia and Republica, irrespective of their initial stance, agree to the terms laid down by

IPO. Result: Peaceful coexistence under international oversight.

Sanctions Imposed: One of the countries decides on aggression, leading IPO to impose sanctions. Result: The aggressor faces economic challenges, leading to internal pressures to revert to a peaceful stance.

Explanations

The Peace-War game, in a political context, isn't just about immediate decisions but also about long-term strategic implications. Every move carries weight, from economic repercussions to public opinion shifts within the countries.

For Democracia: While extending a peace treaty can open trade routes and bolster its economy, the decision is also influenced by internal political pressures and the historical context with Republica.

For Republica: The decision to reciprocate a peace treaty or mobilize troops isn't merely strategic but also stems from nationalistic sentiments and the perceived benefits of territorial expansion.

For IPO: Their involvement isn't just altruistic. Regional stability can have global implications, affecting international trade, migration, and alliances.

In this complex interplay, the Peace-War Game exemplifies that international politics isn't binary but is a spectrum of decisions, each echoing with myriad consequences. The hope, in any such scenario, is that peace and cooperation trump aggression and conflict.

Chapter 12

The Volunteer Dilemma

"In the intricate weave of negotiations, the Volunteer's Dilemma underscores the tension between individual sacrifice and collective gain, reminding us that the thread of shared benefit often relies on the courage of a singular strand."

Introduction

In the multifaceted world of game theory, the Volunteer's Dilemma presents an intriguing examination of collective action problems.

Focusing on the tension between individual and group benefits, this game becomes particularly illuminating when exploring negotiations, casting light on cooperation, altruism, and the dynamics of collective decision-making.

Game Structure and Social Implications

The Volunteer's Dilemma is structured around a scenario where a group benefits from at least one individual volunteering, but at a cost to the volunteer. If no one volunteers, the entire group faces negative consequences.

The game's inherent tension lies in the juxtaposition of individual sacrifice for collective gain.

From a social standpoint, this game highlights:

Altruism vs. Self-Interest: Individuals face the choice of taking a personal hit for the greater good or avoiding cost in the hopes that someone else will volunteer.

Free Riding: If everyone hopes someone else will bear the burden, the group may end up facing detrimental outcomes, underscoring the problem of free riders in group dynamics.

Collective Action Problems in Negotiations

Shared Responsibilities: In team negotiations, members might hope someone else prepares the necessary data or takes the lead, leading to potential unpreparedness if everyone adopts this mindset.

Group Projects and Contributions: In collective ventures, participants might hope others will invest more time, resources, or capital, potentially jeopardizing the project's success.

Shared Sacrifices: In situations demanding collective concessions, like salary cuts to prevent layoffs, individuals might hope others will volunteer, risking more significant collective losses.

Strategies to Encourage Volunteering

Incentivizing Volunteering: Providing incentives, either through rewards or recognition, can motivate individuals to volunteer.

Clear Communication: Ensuring group members understand the collective consequences of non-volunteering can foster a sense of responsibility. Rotational Responsibilities: Instituting a system where volunteering responsibilities rotate ensures that the burden is shared over time.

Building a Culture of Cooperation: Cultivating a team or organizational culture that values cooperation and collective well-being can intrinsically motivate individuals to volunteer.

Practical Exercises & Analysis

Role-Playing the Volunteer's Dilemma

Engage participants in scenarios mirroring the game, then analyze outcomes to understand decision-making patterns and the influence of group dynamics.

Negotiation Simulations with Collective Action Elements

Create negotiation scenarios where the success of the negotiation hinges on members volunteering for specific roles or making sacrifices.

Post-negotiation debriefs can offer insights into the strategies employed and the interplay of individual and collective interests.

Case Study Exploration

Dive into real-world scenarios-like union negotiations, community projects, or international agreements-that echo the Volunteer's Dilemma. These case studies can illuminate the challenges and solutions inherent in collective action negotiations.

Conclusion

The Volunteer's Dilemma, while a structured game, captures the essence of a pervasive challenge in negotiations and group dynamics-the tension between individual costs and collective benefits. As groups navigate the complexities of collective action, understanding the intricacies of this game provides invaluable insights.

It serves as a reminder of the importance of fostering cooperation, clear communication, and a shared sense of responsibility in the delicate dance of negotiations.

Volunteer's Dilemma Practical Application and Analysis

Franchise Agreement: The Volunteer's Dilemma Among Fast-Food Franchisees

Scenario

The buzz of fast food is omnipresent. Among the giants is a renowned fast-food chain, which has given entrepreneurial opportunities to many through its franchise model.

To bolster sales and brand visibility, the idea of a communal advertising fund emerges. Every franchisee has a choice: contribute to the fund and bear the costs or abstain and still potentially benefit from the advertising's ripple effect.

However, if no one steps up, the advertising campaign might never see the light of day, leaving sales stagnant.

Game Setup

Players: Each Franchisee (For simplicity, consider two

franchisees: Franchisee A & Franchisee B)

Choices

- o Contribute to the Advertising Fund (Contribute)

- o   Refrain from Contributing (Refrain)

Payoff Matrix (Described in terms of profitability/enhanced sales for Franchisee A and Franchisee B):

	Franchisee B Contributes	**Franchisee B Refrains**
Franchisee A Contributes	Mutual Boost in Sales (High, High) but Shared Costs (Medium, Medium)	Franchisee A Bears Cost but Both Benefit (Medium, High)
Franchisee A Refrains	Franchisee B Bears Cost but Both Benefit (High, Medium)	No Advertisement, Stagnant Sales (Low, Low)

Explanation of Outcomes

Both Contribute (Contribute, Contribute):
- o   Both franchisees, recognizing the collective benefit, decide to invest in the advertising fund.
- o   Implications for Both: The ensuing advertisement boosts sales for both. While profits rise, both have to bear the advertising costs, making the net profit medium.

Franchisee A Contributes, Franchisee B Refrains (Contribute, Refrain):
- o   Franchisee A invests in the advertising fund, while Franchisee B decides to save costs.

- o Implications for Franchisee A: They bear the advertising costs alone, but the sales increase. The net profit is medium.
- o Implications for Franchisee B: They benefit from the advertisement-induced sales boost without incurring any costs, leading to high profit.

Franchisee A Refrains, Franchisee B Contributes (Refrain, Contribute):

- o Franchisee B invests in the advertising, while Franchisee A avoids the costs.
- o Implications for Franchisee B: They bear the advertising costs alone. While sales rise, the net profit is medium.
- o Implications for Franchisee A: They experience a sales boost without any advertising expenses, enjoying high profit.

Both Refrain (Refrain, Refrain):

- o Both franchisees, possibly expecting the other to shoulder the burden, decide not to contribute.
- o Implications for Both: The advertisement campaign doesn't take off. Without the marketing boost, sales remain stagnant, and both experience low profitability.

Strategic Implications

The Volunteer's Dilemma in this context highlights the tension between individual rationality and collective benefit.

Trust, communication, and past collaboration

experiences can influence franchisees' decisions. The corporate entity (fast-food chain) might need to implement incentives or mechanisms to encourage more franchisees to contribute.

Conclusion

In the competitive world of fast food, the franchisees of this chain find themselves in a classic Volunteer's Dilemma. The allure of shared success through a collective advertisement campaign is evident, but the route to achieving it is fraught with individual calculations and considerations.

While the immediate profitability might be a driving factor, the long-term implications on trust, collaboration, and mutual growth should not be understated. In this game of strategy and cooperation, the franchisees' choices will determine not just their sales figures but also the strength and harmony of their collective enterprise.

Volunteer's Dilemma Practical Application and Analysis

Community Project Funding: The Volunteer's Dilemma in Building a Park

Scenario

The sun casts its golden rays across Greentown, where residents dream of a lush, green park. The community cherishes the idea of a tranquil space for picnics, children's laughter, and morning jogs.

But this dream comes with a price tag. Each resident faces a choice: contribute funds for the park or rely on others to do so. While everyone will benefit from the park, the onus of funding weighs heavily on those who step forward.

Game Setup

Players: Every individual member of Greentown (for simplicity, we'll consider them as a collective group)

Choices:
Contribute (C)
Do Not Contribute (DNC)

Outcome Matrix:

	Majority Contributes	Minority Contributes	No One Contributes
Individual Contributes	Personal Cost, Park Built (Low Burden)	Personal Cost, Park Built (High Burden)	Personal Cost, No Park
Individual Doesn't Contribute	No Personal Cost, Park Built	No Personal Cost, Park Built	No Personal Cost, No Park

Explanation of Outcomes

Majority Contributes:
- o When the majority of the community members choose to fund the project, the financial burden per individual is relatively low, as the cost is spread out.
- o Individual Contributes: A member who contributes feels a personal cost but experiences a low burden as many share it. They also get the reward of the park.
- o Individual Doesn't Contribute: A non-contributing member enjoys the park without any personal financial input.

Minority Contributes:
- o When only a few members decide to fund the park, these few bear a higher financial burden.
- o Individual Contributes: A member who contributes feels a hefty personal cost due to the fewer contributors, but they still get the

reward of the park.
- o Individual Doesn't Contribute: A non-contributing member enjoys the benefits of the park without any personal cost, but at the expense of the few contributors.

No One Contributes:
- o If no community member steps forward with funds, the dream of the park fades away.
- o Both contributors and non-contributors do not benefit from a park, but individuals also don't experience any personal financial loss.

Strategic Implications

The Volunteer's Dilemma highlights the tension between individual interests and collective well-being. Each Greentown member must weigh the personal cost of contributing against the communal benefit of the park.

If everyone acts solely in personal interest, the collective suffers, and the park remains a distant dream.

If some altruistic members take on the heavy burden, the community benefits, but this approach might seem unfair to the contributors.

Conclusion

The quest to fund a community park in Greentown encapsulates the challenges of public goods and communal projects. The Volunteer's Dilemma, as applied to this scenario, underscores the interplay between personal sacrifices and collective rewards. For Greentown to blossom with greenery and laughter, it requires not just funds but a coming together of community spirit, shared dreams, and an understanding of the larger good.

Chapter 13

The Game of Chicken

"In the Game of Chicken, where risk meets bravado on the precipice of decision, game theory doesn't just chart possible outcomes but unveils the intricate dancebetween courage and consequence."

Introduction

Game theory, the study of strategic interaction among rational decision-makers, offers a rich tapestry of scenarios that model various real-life situations. One such game that has intrigued scholars, strategists, and even popular culture enthusiasts is the Game of Chicken.

This chapter delves into the origins, dynamics, and implications of this game.

Origins of the Game

The Game of Chicken draws its name from a daredevil challenge where two drivers speed towards each other on a collision course. The first driver to swerve is dubbed the "chicken," indicating a loss of nerve, while the other emerges as the victor.

If neither swerves, both crash, leading to a mutually disastrous outcome. This dangerous stunt, while often associated with rebellious youth in movies, provides a fascinating model for certain kinds of strategic interactions.

Dynamics and Strategies

In the Game of Chicken, both players have two options: to "swerve" or to "stay." The payoffs are structured such that the worst outcome for each player is to stay while the other swerves.

The second-worst outcome is for both to crash by staying the course. The third in rank is both choosing to swerve, while the most favorable outcome is to have the opponent swerve while one stays.

The game captures a paradox

While mutual cooperation (both swerving) is preferable to mutual non-cooperation (both crashing), the individual temptation to risk and emerge as the "brave" one, expecting the other to swerve, can lead to catastrophe.

Implications Beyond Daredevilry

International Relations: Nuclear arms races during the Cold War had elements of the Game of Chicken. Neither superpower wanted a nuclear war (analogous to crashing), but neither wanted to be the first to disarm unilaterally (being the "chicken").

Business: Competitive strategies, especially in oligopolistic markets, can mirror the Game of Chicken. Companies might escalate aggressive pricing or marketing campaigns hoping their rivals will back down, but risking mutual losses if none relent.

Negotiations: Two parties might hold out, hoping the other will make concessions. If neither party concedes, both might lose out on a potentially beneficial agreement.

Resolving the Game

Several strategies have been proposed to "win" the Game of Chicken or to avoid the disastrous crash: Commitment Tactics: One player can signal their intent not to swerve, maybe by visibly breaking their steering wheel. This forces the other player into the role of the responder.

Randomization

Players can randomize their strategies, making them unpredictable and forcing the game into a mixed strategy equilibrium.
Repetition and Reputation: If the Game of Chicken is played repeatedly, players can build reputations, which might influence future plays.

Conclusion

The Game of Chicken provides valuable insights into scenarios where risk, reward, and bravado intersect. While the game's structure is simple, its real-world manifestations are complex, highlighting the intricacies of strategic decision-making.

As with many game theory models, while they offer a theoretical framework, real-world outcomes depend on myriad factors, including human emotions, irrationality, and unpredictability. The Game of

Chicken serves as a stark reminder of the high stakes involved in certain decisions and the thin line between victory and disaster.

Chicken Practical Application and Analysis

Foreign Diplomacy: Using The Game of Chicken

Scenario

Two powerful nations, Atlantica and Pacifica, find themselves in a territorial dispute over a newly discovered island located equidistant from their shores.

The island is rich in rare minerals, making it a valuable asset. Both nations send naval fleets to stake their claim, resulting in a tense standoff. Neither wants to appear weak on the global stage, but a direct military conflict would be disastrous for both. The international community is watching closely.

Players:

Atlantica
Pacifica

Options

Atlantica:
- o Advance: Move their naval fleet closer to the island, increasing tensions.
- o Retreat: Withdraw a portion of their fleet, indicating a willingness to negotiate.
- o Propose Neutral Mediation: Offer to have a neutral nation mediate the dispute.

Pacifica:
- o Advance: Position their naval fleet more aggressively, potentially triggering conflict.
- o Retreat: Pull back some of their naval presence, signaling a potential compromise.
- o Accept Mediation: Agree to third-party mediation, deescalating the situation.

Possible Outcomes

Mutual Aggression: Both Atlantica and Pacifica advance, resulting in a high-sea standoff that can escalate to a military conflict. This outcome risks international condemnation and potential loss for both nations.

One-Sided Aggression (Atlantica): Atlantica advances while Pacifica retreats. Atlantica appears dominant, but Pacifica gains global sympathy, potentially leading to international pressure on Atlantica.

One-Sided Aggression (Pacifica): Pacifica advances aggressively while Atlantica proposes neutral mediation. The global community views Atlantica as the peacemaker and Pacifica as the aggressor, potentially resulting in sanctions or diplomatic isolation for Pacifica.

Mutual Deescalation: Both nations retreat, leading to a tacit understanding. While the immediate crisis is averted, the long-term status of the island remains uncertain.

Mediated Settlement: One nation proposes mediation, and the other accepts. The neutral nation's mediation results in a shared agreement on the island's usage, ensuring peace and mutual benefit.

Explanations

The Game of Chicken, in this diplomatic scenario, encapsulates the tension between national pride and the potential catastrophic consequences of military conflict:

For Atlantica: Advancing is a show of strength but risks conflict and global backlash. Proposing neutral mediation, while appearing as a peaceful move, can also be a strategy to diplomatically isolate Pacifica if they refuse.

For Pacifica: An aggressive stance can be a symbol of national resolve but can also plunge the nation into an unwanted conflict. Retreating, on the other hand, might seem like a temporary setback but can be a strategic move to gain international support.

In this intricate dance of power and diplomacy, the Game of Chicken underscores the delicate balance nations tread on the global stage, where decisions aren't merely about immediate gains but about long-term geopolitical standing and strategy.

Chicken Practical Application and Analysis

Foreclosure: Using The Game of Chicken

Scenario

In a tight-knit community, two homeowners, Alice and Bob, have had a long-standing personal feud. Alice lent Bob a significant amount of money a few years back, using his house as collateral.

With the debt unpaid and reaching its due date, Alice threatens to foreclose on Bob's house. Bob, sensing an opportunity to challenge Alice's claim, considers dragging the matter to court, which could tarnish both their reputations in the community.

As the deadline approaches, both have to decide whether to escalate the matter or find a compromise, knowing that mutual intransigence can lead to financial and social repercussions for both.

Players:
Alice
Bob

Options

Alice:
- Foreclose: Take aggressive action and initiate the foreclosure process on Bob's house.
- Negotiate: Offer terms for a structured debt repayment or a possible discount on the

amount.

Bob:
- o Challenge: Drag the matter to court, potentially airing personal grievances publicly.
- o Settle: Find a way to meet the obligations, possibly asking for more time or reduced terms.

Possible Outcomes

Mutual Aggression: Alice chooses to foreclose, and Bob takes the matter to court. Both undergo financial strain due to legal costs, and their personal reputations suffer in the community.

One-Sided Aggression (Alice): Alice initiates foreclosure, but Bob decides to settle. Bob loses his house, leading to personal and financial strain, while Alice gains the property but is viewed as aggressive by community members.

One-Sided Aggression (Bob): Alice offers a negotiated term, but Bob chooses to challenge it in court. The drawn-out legal battle strains Alice's resources and patience, while Bob risks losing more money and the house.

Mutual Cooperation: Alice and Bob mutually decide to renegotiate the terms. Bob secures more time or better repayment conditions, while Alice ensures her money is returned without community fallout.

Explanations

In this personal rendition of the Game of Chicken, the stakes are not just financial but deeply emotional and social:

- o For Alice: Foreclosing on Bob's house is not just about recovering her money but also asserting her dominance in the personal feud. However, by doing so, she risks alienation in the community and potential legal complications. Choosing to negotiate displays maturity, ensuring financial return and preserving her community standing.

- o For Bob: Challenging Alice by taking the matter to court is a show of resistance against what he perceives as Alice's high-handedness. It offers a chance of keeping his house but risks financial ruin and public airing of personal disputes. Settling the debt might feel like a personal defeat, but it ensures his financial and social stability.

The dynamics of this Game of Chicken highlight that personal relationships, when mixed with financial dealings, can complicate decisions.

The game's outcomes serve as a stark reminder of the intertwining of pride, finances, and reputation in personal disputes. The hope, as always in such conflicts, is that both parties realize the broader implications of their decisions and choose cooperation over conflict.

Chapter 14

The Game of Trust

"In the Game of Trust, the currency isn't just money but the delicate interplay of faith and reciprocity; it's where game theory meets the heart's ledger."

Introduction

Game theory, an interdisciplinary field spanning economics, political science, and psychology, offers profound insights into how individuals make decisions in interactive scenarios.

While many games like the Prisoner's Dilemma or the Game of Chicken analyze choices under conflict and competition, the Game of Trust introduces us to an aspect foundational to human society which is trustworthiness.

Origins and Structure of the Game

The Game of Trust, sometimes referred to as the Trust Game or the Investment Game, was developed to understand the dynamics of trust and reciprocity in decision-making. Two players participate in this game.

The first player, the "trustor," is given a sum of money. They can choose to keep it or send part or all of it to the second player, the "trustee." Money sent gets multiplied (usually doubled or tripled) by the experimenter before the trustee receives it. The trustee then decides how much of this multiplied amount to send back to the trustor.

Analyzing the Dynamics

The trustor faces the dilemma of whether to trust the trustee. Sending money implies trust but also vulnerability because the trustee might keep all the money. For the trustee, the game poses the question of reciprocity: should they honor the trustor's faith and send money back, or maximize their own benefit by keeping it?

Implications from Experimental Findings

Nature of Trust: Experimental results from various trust games show that individuals tend to trust even when facing potential losses, suggesting an innate human tendency to trust.

Reciprocity and Fairness: A significant proportion of trustees, when trusted, reciprocate by sending money back. This behavior suggests that considerations of fairness and positive reciprocity influence decision-making.

Cultural Differences: Cross-cultural experiments with the trust game have found variations in trust and reciprocity levels across different societies, indicating cultural norms and values play a role in decision-making.

Broader Applications and Relevance

Business Relations: Trust is foundational in business, especially in long-term partnerships. A business placing an order with a new supplier or a company investing in employee training are real-world analogies of the trust game.

Personal Relationships: Trust and reciprocity are pillars of personal relationships, be it friendships, family ties, or romantic partnerships.

Societal Dynamics: Trust in public institutions, government policies, or communal leaders can be framed within the context of the trust game. The response of these entities then dictates societal perception and future trust levels.

Conclusion

The Game of Trust, through its elegant structure, shines a light on the intricate interplay of trust and reciprocity in human interactions. It underscores the idea that while economic theories often assume individuals act to maximize their personal gain, real-world decisions are influenced by a mix of self-interest, intrinsic values, societal norms, and relational dynamics.

In the vast landscape of game theory, the Trust Game stands as a testament to the depth of human complexity, emphasizing the need to incorporate psychological and sociological perspectives when deciphering human behavior.

Trust Practical Application and Analysis

Personal Relationship: Using The Game of Trust

Scenario

Two close friends, Emily and Sarah, have had a falling out over a misunderstanding. Emily believes that Sarah spoke behind her back, while Sarah insists it was an innocent comment taken out of context.

Both value their long-standing friendship but are hurt by recent events. They face a decision: should they approach each other to discuss and clarify the misunderstanding or wait for the other to take the initiative, risking further strain in the relationship?

Players:
Emily
Sarah

Options:

Emily:
- o Approach: Initiate a conversation with Sarah to address the issue and clarify misunderstandings.
- o Wait: Decide not to initiate and wait for Sarah to make the first move, displaying a stance of being the 'wronged' party.
- o Seek Mediation: Suggest a mutual friend to mediate the conversation, hoping for a neutral

perspective.

Sarah:
- o Approach: Reach out to Emily, apologizing and explaining her side of the story.
- o Wait: Hold back, hoping Emily will realize the misunderstanding and come forward.
- o Accept Mediation: Agree to a mediated conversation if Emily proposes it.

Possible Outcomes

Mutual Approach: Both Emily and Sarah decide to talk it out, leading to quick resolution, understanding, and a strengthened bond.

One-Sided Approach (Emily): Emily approaches Sarah while Sarah waits. The conversation might resolve the issue, but Sarah may feel she's in a position of power since Emily initiated.

One-Sided Approach (Sarah): Sarah takes the initiative, while Emily holds back. The dynamic is similar to the previous outcome, but roles reversed.

Mutual Wait: Both decide to wait for the other to take the initiative, leading to prolonged strain, potential gossip among friends, and a deteriorating relationship.

Mediated Discussion: Either Emily proposes mediation or Sarah agrees to it when proposed. A neutral friend helps in addressing grievances, ensuring both sides feel heard. This can lead to resolution or, at the very least, clarity on where each stands.

Explanations

In this adaptation of the Game of Trust, the stakes are emotional rather than material:

For Emily: Taking the initiative to approach Sarah is a vulnerable move, symbolizing trust and the value she places on the relationship. Waiting might seem like a protective move but risks making the rift wider. Proposing mediation shows a willingness to resolve issues but with support.

For Sarah: Initiating the conversation displays maturity and a desire for resolution. However, waiting might be a test of Emily's commitment to the friendship.

The dynamics of this Game of Trust reveal the intricacies of personal relationships, where actions aren't just about immediate resolution but about underlying emotions, trust, and the balance of power in friendships.

It underscores that in personal relationships, often the most challenging step is taking the initiative, signaling trust and a desire for reconciliation.

Trust Practical Application and Analysis

Corporate Takeover: Using The Game of Trust

Scenario

Two major tech companies, TechnoGlobal and CyberCorp, are in initial talks for a potential merger. Both companies possess critical trade secrets and patented technologies that could significantly benefit the other. The dilemma arises when both contemplate whether to reveal these confidential assets during the negotiation phase to facilitate a smooth merger or keep them hidden to ensure a competitive edge if merger talks fail.

Players:
TechnoGlobal
CyberCorp

Options:

TechnoGlobal:
- o Reveal: Disclose critical trade secrets and patented information to CyberCorp to demonstrate good faith.
- o Conceal: Hold back confidential information, indicating caution and protectiveness.
- o Propose NDA: Suggest both parties sign a Non-Disclosure Agreement to ensure any shared information remains confidential, regardless of merger outcomes.

CyberCorp:
- o Reveal: Share their proprietary information with TechnoGlobal, hoping for mutual trust.
- o Conceal: Withhold vital information, signaling a guarded stance.
- o Accept NDA: Agree to TechnoGlobal's proposal for an NDA, indicating willingness to share but with legal safeguards.

Possible Outcomes

Mutual Revelation: Both TechnoGlobal and CyberCorp reveal their secrets, leading to a comprehensive understanding, boosting trust, and making the merger process smoother.

One-Sided Revelation (TechnoGlobal): TechnoGlobal reveals while CyberCorp conceals. This might give CyberCorp an immediate advantage, but it may be perceived as a breach of trust, complicating merger negotiations.

One-Sided Revelation (CyberCorp): CyberCorp opens up, while TechnoGlobal remains guarded. The dynamics are similar to the above but with roles reversed.

Mutual Concealment: Both companies decide to withhold information. This leads to a prolonged negotiation phase, with both parties constantly second-guessing and analyzing the other's intent. NDA-Based Sharing:

Either TechnoGlobal proposes or CyberCorp accepts the NDA. Both parties share confidential information under legal protection, ensuring trust is upheld and proprietary secrets remain safeguarded.

Explanations

In this corporate adaptation of the Game of Trust, stakes are high, with significant financial implications:

For TechnoGlobal: Revealing trade secrets showcases a commitment to the merger and can speed up the process. However, if CyberCorp doesn't reciprocate, TechnoGlobal risks losing its competitive advantage. Proposing an NDA is a middle-ground strategy, blending trust with caution.

For CyberCorp: Sharing proprietary information can be a powerful gesture of trust, yet concealment might be seen as a strategic, albeit risk-averse, move. Agreeing to an NDA suggests a willingness to cooperate but within a secure framework.

This game illuminates the subtle dance of corporate negotiations, where decisions aren't merely about immediate gains but are deeply intertwined with long-term strategy, trust-building, and risk assessment. It underscores that in high-stakes corporate environments, balancing transparency with protection can be a challenging yet crucial endeavor.

Chapter 15

The Stag Hunt

"In the intricate dance of negotiation, the Stag Hunt of game theory reminds us that the richest rewards often lie in the realm of trust and collaboration, yet the path to them ispaved with risks and choices."

Negotiation, in its essence, is about parties coming together to find a mutually beneficial resolution to conflicting interests. The dynamics of cooperation and competition, trust, and risk, are played out on this interactive stage. Game theory, the study of strategic interplay between rational decision-makers, provides powerful models to dissect these dynamics. One such model, with profound relevance to the world of negotiation, is the 'Stag Hunt'.

Origins and Overview of the Stag Hunt

Attributed to philosopher Jean-Jacques Rousseau, the Stag Hunt presents a situation where two hunters must decide between collaborating to hunt a stag or working independently to catch rabbits.

While the stag offers a greater reward, it demands cooperation. A rabbit, on the other hand, is less rewarding but is a guaranteed catch irrespective of the other hunter's choice. The dilemma? Choosing the stag, and the promise of a bigger prize, hinges on trust that the other hunter will do the same.

Stag Hunt and Negotiation Dynamics

Mutual Cooperation for Maximum Gain: At its core, the Stag Hunt accentuates the potential benefits of collaboration. In negotiations, this translates to parties working together, sharing resources, and exchanging information to reach an optimal solution that benefits all. However, this cooperation often requires a leap of faith.

Risk Assessment and Trust: The decision to 'hunt the stag' is inherently risky. In a negotiation, this might involve sharing proprietary information, agreeing to a compromise, or making a significant upfront investment. Such decisions rest heavily on the trustworthiness of the other party. If this trust is misplaced, one stands to lose, just as the lone stag hunter would leave empty-handed.

Safety in Conservatism: Opting for the rabbit signifies a conservative approach, minimizing risks. In negotiation parlance, this could mean settling for a less favorable but guaranteed outcome, not sharing critical data, or avoiding novel but uncertain strategies.

Communication as a Game-Changer: In the Stag Hunt, if the hunters could effectively communicate, they could potentially ensure they both opt for the stag. Similarly, clear communication in negotiations can mitigate misunderstandings, build trust, and pave the way for collaborative solutions.

Real-World Implications in Negotiations

Business Partnerships: Companies deliberating on joint ventures face a stag hunt scenario. Both might benefit immensely from pooling resources (the stag). Yet, concerns about the other company not committing fully might lead to a more conservative, individual approach (the rabbit).

Trade and Diplomatic Agreements: Countries negotiating trade pacts confront similar dilemmas. Mutual concessions can lead to a prosperous agreement (the stag), but fears about non-compliance or future breaches might result in guarded, less beneficial agreements (the rabbit).

Dispute Resolutions: Parties in a legal or territorial dispute can either collaborate for a swift, mutually beneficial resolution (the stag) or tread a more prolonged, resource-intensive path, ensuring minimal personal loss (the rabbit).

Conclusion

The Stag Hunt, through its seemingly simple narrative, offers profound insights into the complexities of negotiations. It encapsulates the age-old tug-of-war between individual safety and collective gain, between trust and caution.

As negotiators, understanding the underpinnings of the Stag Hunt equips us to better navigate decisions, assess risks, and build trust, ultimately guiding us towards more fruitful, collaborative outcomes.

Stag Hunt Practical Application and Analysis

Hotel Purchase: Using The Game of Stag Hunt

Scenario

Real estate moguls, Jackson and Caroline, have both set their eyes on the luxurious Grand Serenity Hotel located in a prime vacation spot. The current owner of the hotel has expressed interest in selling, but for a price that is slightly above market rate due to the hotel's reputation and location.

Jackson has the funds to buy it outright, but wonders if pooling resources with Caroline could be beneficial for further expansion. Caroline, on the other hand, has extensive hotel management experience and connections that could boost the hotel's profits even higher, but she can't afford the full purchase on her own.

The "stag" here represents both Jackson and Caroline teaming up to buy and run the hotel, potentially maximizing its potential. The "rabbit" symbolizes the less rewarding but safer option of trying to acquire or benefit from the hotel individually.

Players:
Jackson
Caroline
Grand Serenity Hotel Owner

Options

Jackson:
- o Buy Hotel Outright: Gain full control, but miss out on Caroline's expertise.
- o Partner with Caroline: Split the purchase cost, and benefit from Caroline's hotel management experience.
- o Negotiate Price: Try to get the hotel for a lower price but risk losing it to another buyer.

Caroline:
- o Seek External Funding: Try to buy the hotel without Jackson but might end up in debt or give away significant equity.
- o Partner with Jackson: Contribute her management expertise in exchange for a share in ownership.
- o Offer Management Services: If she can't buy, offer her expertise to whoever acquires the hotel, ensuring a stake in its success.

Grand Serenity Hotel Owner:
- o Sell to the Highest Bidder: Irrespective of their plans for the hotel.
- o Consider Future of the Hotel: Choose a buyer who will maintain the hotel's reputation, even if the offer is slightly lower.
- o Hold onto the Property: Wait for better offers or consider not selling at all.

Outcomes

Both Jackson and Caroline go solo (Rabbit-Rabbit):
Jackson might acquire the property but may not maximize its profit potential without Caroline's expertise. Caroline, unable to buy, might look elsewhere or merely offer her services.

Jackson goes solo, Caroline offers expertise (Rabbit-Stag):
Jackson gets the property, but Caroline doesn't benefit from ownership. However, the hotel thrives under her management.

Jackson and Caroline collaborate (Stag-Stag):
They pool resources, acquire the hotel, and it reaches unprecedented success due to their combined financial and management prowess.

Caroline seeks external funding, Jackson backs out (Stag-Rabbit):
Caroline manages to buy the hotel but is saddled with debt or gives away significant equity. Jackson misses out on the potential success of the hotel.

The Stag Hunt beautifully captures the tension in this scenario. Both Jackson and Caroline stand to gain the most by cooperating, but it requires a leap of trust and the possibility of missing out on individual goals. This game encapsulates many real-world decisions, where collaboration might be the most rewarding option but requires a delicate balance of trust, communication, and shared vision.

Stag Hunt Practical Application and Analysis

Private Car Sale: Using The Game of Stag Hunt

Scenario

Hannah is looking to sell her classic vintage car, which has both sentimental and monetary value. She has two potential buyers, Marcus and Laura. Marcus is an avid car collector and recognizes the unique value of the car, while Laura is looking for a stylish, reliable vehicle but isn't as emotionally attached to it as Marcus.

Both Marcus and Laura can offer a high price in hopes of securing the car, or they can bid low to try and get a bargain. Hannah, meanwhile, can either set a fixed price or leave it open for negotiation, in hopes of driving up the price.

The "stag" represents a scenario where the buyer offers a high price, which is mutually beneficial for both the seller (gets a high price) and the buyer (secures a valuable car). The "rabbit" is the safer, less rewarding option, where the buyer offers a low price, hoping to get a bargain.

Players:
Hannah (Seller)
Marcus (Buyer)
Laura (Buyer)

Options:

Hannah:
- o Set a Fixed Price: Offer clarity and security but might deter potential higher bids.
- o Open for Negotiation: Risky, but the competitive spirit might drive up the price, especially if both buyers are keen.

Marcus:
- o High Bid: Secure the car, recognizing its unique value but at a premium cost.
- o Low Bid: Try to get a bargain, but risk losing the car to a higher bidder.

Laura:
- o High Bid: Secure a stylish, reliable car even if it's at a higher price.
- o Low Bid: Aim for a bargain, but risk missing out.

Outcomes

Both Marcus and Laura bid high (Stag-Stag):
A bidding war ensues. Hannah stands to gain the most, achieving a price at the higher end of the car's value. The car goes to the highest bidder.

Marcus bids high, Laura bids low (Stag-Rabbit):
Marcus secures the car, recognizing its unique value. Laura misses out, but she tried for a bargain. Hannah gets a satisfactory price for the car.

Laura bids high, Marcus bids low (Stag-Rabbit):
Laura secures the car, paying a premium. Marcus misses out on adding the unique car to his collection. Hannah gets a good price.

Both Marcus and Laura bid low (Rabbit-Rabbit):
Hannah faces a dilemma: sell the car at a lower price or hold out in hopes of a better offer in the future. Either Marcus or Laura might get the car at a bargain.

In this Stag Hunt scenario, trust and assessment of the other party's intentions play a crucial role. Both buyers must gauge not only the seller's expectations but also the competing buyer's strategy. The tension between collaborative mutual benefit and individual security is at the heart of this classic game theory scenario, exemplified in the context of a private car sale.

Chapter 16
Key Takeaways

"In the vast theater of real-world negotiations, game theory serves as the compass, guiding us through the intricate dance of choices, outcomes, and shared destinies."

Game theory, a realm of strategic thought and decision-making, is deeply intertwined with the realities of negotiations in diverse domains. From the intricacies of business mergers to the delicate balance in diplomatic talks and the intense dynamics of real estate, game theory provides invaluable insights into the art of negotiation. Delving into the various games discussed, from the Prisoner's Dilemma to the Volunteer's Dilemma, we extract key learnings that guide negotiators in real-world situations.

1. Power Dynamics and Asymmetry:

Games like the Dictator Game, seen in salary negotiations, and the Volunteer's Dilemma in community funding highlight the imbalances of power. While one party may hold more power or leverage, game theory teaches us that even the most powerful entities should consider long-term impacts, reputation, and relationships over immediate gains. Unilateral decisions, while effective in the short run, may erode trust in the long run.

2. The Balance of Cooperation and Competition:

The Prisoner's Dilemma in lease agreements or the Peace-War Game in diplomatic talks showcases the perpetual tension between individual interest and collective good. While it might seem rational to act in self-interest, the larger payoff often lies in cooperative strategies that enhance mutual trust and yield shared benefits.

3. The Risk of Stalemates:

Deadlocks, as seen in labor union bargains, emphasize the dangerous territory of intractable positions. Stalemates can lead to suboptimal outcomes for all parties involved. Introducing third-party mediators or altering the negotiation environment can help in breaking the impasse.

4. Predictive Play and Strategic Adaptation:

The Matching Penny game in contract negotiations or the Cournot Competition in divorce settlements underscores the importance of predicting an opponent's move and adjusting one's strategy. Flexibility and the ability to adapt based on the perceived moves of the other party can lead to advantageous outcomes.

5. The Importance of Communication and Signaling:

In games like the Battle of the Sexes, applied to trade agreements, effective communication emerges as paramount. Misunderstandings can lead to inefficient outcomes, while clear signaling and open dialogue can pave the way for mutually beneficial resolutions.

6. Incremental Decision Making:

The Centipede Game in real estate dealings sheds light on the nature of sequential decision-making. At every juncture, parties must weigh the benefits of continuation against the risks, considering not just immediate outcomes but also future implications.

7. The Role of External Factors:

Games like the Cournot Competition, applied to vendor agreements or market price settings, remind us that external market forces, governmental regulations, public sentiment, and unforeseen events play a substantial role in determining the payoff of a given strategy.

8. The Value of Reputation and Long-term Relations:

The Traveler's Dilemma in car purchases or the Dictator Game in salary negotiations underscore the intangible yet invaluable assets of reputation and trust. Parties that act fairly, even if it means short-term sacrifices, often enjoy long-term benefits in terms of loyalty, repeat business, and positive word of mouth.

Conclusion

Game theory is not just mathematical models and theoretical constructs; it's a lens to understand, navigate, and optimize the intricate dance of negotiations in our interconnected world. Each game, with its unique setup and outcomes, offers nuggets of wisdom.

When negotiators, whether they're diplomats, CEOs, or everyday consumers, apply these insights, they are better equipped to navigate complex decisions, foster beneficial relationships, and achieve outcomes that resonate with both individual aspirations and collective progress.